TREATISE
ON
THE COURT

EUSTACHE DE REFUGE

TREATISE
ON
THE COURT

*The Early Modern Management Classic
on Organizational Behaviour*

A NEW TRANSLATION BY

J. Chris Cooper

Orgpax Publications, Inc.
7700 Congress Avenue
Boca Raton, FL 33487 USA
http://www.treatiseonthecourt.com

ISBN-13: 978-0-9814544-0-5
ISBN-10: 0-9814544-0-2

Illustrations from the author's collection.
Cover and Interior Design: Desktop Miracles, Inc.
Printed in the United States of America

Publisher's Cataloging-In-Publication Data
(Prepared by The Donohue Group, Inc.)

Refuge, Eustache de, d. 1617.
      [Traicté de la cour. Part 2. English]
      Treatise on the court : the early modern management classic on
organizational behaviour : a new translation / by J. Chris Cooper.
          p. : facsims. ;   cm.
      Translation of Book Two of Traicté de la cour, first published ca.
1616.
      Includes bibliographical references and index.
      ISBN-13: 978-0-9814544-0-5
      ISBN-10: 0-9814544-0-2
      1. Organizational behavior—Early works to 1800.   2. Manage-
ment—Early works to 1800.   3. Courts and courtiers—Early works
to 1800.   4. Favorites, Royal—Early works to 1800.   I. Cooper, J.
Chris (John Christopher), 1943-   II. Title.
HM791 .R4413 2008   302.35

CONTENTS

PREFACE

I came by my interest in early modern management honestly. After many years collecting self-help books on management from less complicated times, I came across a copy of the 1695 edition of *Arcana Aulica, or Walsingham's Manual of Prudential Maxims for the States-Man and Courtier* in G. David's excellent antiquarian book room in Cambridge. Reading it in the aircraft over the Atlantic, I was struck by the relevance of its insights to today's organizational world and decided to buy a few copies of a modern version to share with friends and fellow practitioners. At that point, I discovered not only that there was no modern version available but that *Arcana Aulica* was, even by the looser authorship conventions of the times, in fact one of the more egregious rip-offs of the French original *Treatise on the Court, or the Education of Courtiers* (*Traicté de la cour, ou instruction des courtisans*) by Eustache de Refuge. A reading of the French original revealed an equally fascinating yet crisper text, and this translation was a natural consequence. While it has been going through its many drafts, I have been able to do some preliminary research into the author, the organizational context of the early modern era, and the "courtesy" and then "civility" literary genre of which Eustache de Refuge's work is generally considered a part. The result has been a growing personal interest in this period in the history of organizations and its (largely forgotten) contributions to our understanding of organizational behaviour that I hope others may come to share. Those who are interested may get a taste of the scope of possibilities from the notes at the end of this book or from www.treatiseonthecourt.com.

ACKNOWLEDGEMENTS

This book would not have been possible without the help of several people, both living and dead. While the mistakes are all mine, I would like to thank John Reynolds, and to a lesser extent, Edward Walsingham and Rev. Girolamo Camini for their help interpreting some of the more challenging nuances of Eustache de Refuge's original French. I am also indebted to Kaili Clackson for her help deciphering the logic diagram in the Italian version. A special thanks to my business partner Lydia Szostak for her tireless and "cheerful" text entry and correction of the many iterations and refinements of the manuscript. Erin Stropes deserves a special acknowledgement for her role in the project—not only has her editorial help been invaluable, but her knowledge, research and inquiring mind have contributed information of which I was previously unaware, and many supporting parts of this publication owe much to her drafts. Finally, I acknowledge my lasting debt to my wife, Marie-Claude, whose unquestioning support for my newfound early modern passions has made so much possible.

MONTREAL, 2007

for DLB

INTRODUCTION

OVERVIEW

This is the fifth English translation of Book Two of Eustache de Refuge's management classic *Treatise on the Court, or the Education of Courtiers* (*Traicté de la cour ou instruction des courtisans*), but the first to be published since 1673. Probably first printed in Holland in 1615 or 1616, the *Treatise on the Court* was a pioneering work on organizational behaviour, and its author, Eustache de Refuge,[1] *seigneur de Précy et de Courcelles*, a pioneer executive of the French crown.

Advice on business and management had been published before the seventeenth century,[2] but most of this had been for rulers on how to rule ("mirrors for Princes," the most durable being Machiavelli's *The Prince*) or policies for the management of private banking enterprises such as the Medicis' or those of religious orders. While the origins of organizational behaviour as a topic have been loosely traced to the Renaissance,[3] how-to books dedicated to the subject are generally considered to have begun appearing in the nineteenth century, some 250 years after the first edition of the *Treatise on the Court*. Until now, Eustache de Refuge's work has remained unknown to students of management, having been buried in the plethora of "courtesy" literature[4] that was published in the sixteenth and seventeenth centuries to set social standards for the upper classes.

The *Treatise*, despite its superficial appearance as a cynical, Machiavellian work in fact promotes doing the right thing under all circumstances, while approaching the reality of organizational life at court with unvarnished realism.[5] It also promotes the greater good of the whole over the whims or evil intentions of a leader; a relatively unremarkable notion today, but one that conflicted with the doctrine of absolutism[6] espoused by most monarchs at the time. In fact De Refuge recommends a practical approach to work life that balances courtesy, determination and principles: "*non*-moral rather than *im*moral."[7]

The *Treatise on the Court* appeared originally in two books (*parties*). The first, which is summarized but not reproduced here, follows in the tradition of other courtesy books of the period, laying out the general attributes and behaviours necessary for a successful courtier. The second book breaks with this tradition and outlines the circumstances likely to be encountered by someone making his or her career in a court organization and gives advice on how to deal successfully with specific situations. Pragmatic but strongly value-based, this book of the *Treatise* walks the reader through from a successful career start, to gaining favour and advancement, to maintaining a position of power and influence, and concludes with how to bow out gracefully at career's end. Book Two was always more popular than Book One, probably precisely because of the day-to-day practicality of its advice.

The *Treatise* was written in the early modern era,[8] a time when France was emerging as the largest united power in Europe and laying the foundations of an increasingly centralized administration. De Refuge was by family tradition (and clearly by vocation) admirably positioned to become a key executive in this emerging national enterprise, and his *Treatise* was the product of a long and successful career. It expresses the voice of experience.

De Refuge's work was destined to become a huge best-seller for over a century, running through multiple editions in French, English, Italian, Latin, German, and Dutch. In the absence of copyright laws, great portions were lifted by other authors and their origin rather conveniently forgotten, and uncited editions of Book Two at least were still appearing in the first half of the eighteenth century.

Organizational Context

Royal and princely courts of the sixteenth and seventeenth centuries[9] were not merely places where overdressed and sycophantic courtiers gathered to participate in elaborate balls, masques, hunting expeditions and other diversions. While ostentatious leisure activities were a required feature of every court, the whole machinery of government was also run from there. In fact, court structures in the early modern era were marked by a growing distinction between the structure that ran the household (real estate, catering, stables, leisure activities, etc.) and the organization that ran the burgeoning business of government. On the other hand, there was as yet no distinction between judicial and executive branches, the crown conferring sweeping powers on senior positions and making these top public-service jobs in some ways more akin to executive positions in industry (rather than government) today.

A specialized cadre of administrators, a legal and managerial elite that had been forming in France for two or three generations, carried out the business of government. Highly educated and bound together by self-interest and a network of marriages, many of these families had parlayed commercial fortunes made in the sixteenth century into social status as "nobles of the robe" (*noblesse de la robe*).[10] They achieved this transformation over time through the purchase of administrative offices and land, through living nobly (civilly and expensively), through providing first-rate education for their sons, through the documentation of their (sometimes dubious) noble lineages, and through the judicious use of their wealth to circumvent a few of the rules. Generally looked down on by the old "nobles of the sword" (*noblesse de l'épée*) whose established power they threatened, this new nobility hung together and were the group that enabled the French kings to exercise increasing executive control throughout the country, the biggest in Western Europe at the time. These men saw it as their duty to ensure that even the king did not exceed his powers, that justice was meted out, that the taxes necessary to run the state were collected, that armies were raised and that transportation and defense infrastructures across the country were maintained. They also ensured that national (regal) industrial businesses were properly run, that public order was maintained, that relationships with internal regions and foreign states were negotiated and sustained, and generally that the business of the state was run as smoothly as possible. In early modern France[11] this was no small undertaking, as internal religious and territorial wars created almost continuous havoc and ruined national finances.

In this world, the title "prince," as De Refuge used it, applied equally to men and women (queens and queen mothers in particular, such as Catherine de Medici and Marie de Medici[12] during Eustache de Refuge's lifetime) to designate anyone maintaining a court.[13] Each royal prince maintained a court from birth, so at a minimum, there were several princes of royal blood in France at any one time, not to mention the other lesser princes within France and those who ruled over the multitude of other empires, nations, principalities, duchies, dioceses and other jurisdictions that dotted the country's borders.

The status of "noble" was conferred in theory on anyone to whom the monarch delegated any of his or her (absolute) authority, much as the status of "manager" designates a person with delegated authority in a modern organization.

EUSTACHE DE REFUGE

The biography of the author[14] is a matter of continuing research, but enough can be gathered to outline a brilliant career for the French crown, particularly for Henri IV ("The Great") and for Marie de Medici as regent for her son by Henri, Louis XIII.

A brief summary of his life and times appears in the Chronology and is sufficient to illustrate De Refuge's rise to positions of increasing responsibility and the variety of complex projects he undertook in a rapidly changing France and Europe. This experience included familiarity both with centralized monarchical organizations such as those of France and Flanders and with the more nebulous and meritocratic federations of the thirteen cantons of Switzerland and the younger republic of Holland. In the words of an eighteenth-century chronicler, Eustache de

Refuge "was well versed both in the theory and practise of affairs, he having read a vast number of books, and had an extensive and long experience in Courts and the affairs of Kings, Princes, States and Commonwealths, in which the Kings of France had usefully employed him, and . . . they never made the least objection to his wise conduct."[15]

De Refuge gained his organizational experience during a unique window in French history. Before his time, France was so fragmented and wracked by war that the machinery of government was barely able to get by. The government organization was split into many overlapping jurisdictions with varying degrees of autonomy, and management from the center relied heavily on delegation to trusted representatives such as Eustache de Refuge. After his death, the combination of venal government offices (which De Refuge fiercely opposed)[16] becoming hereditary, the growth in size of the French economy and bureaucracy and the centralization of the reins of administrative power under Richelieu and Mazarin moved the state organization more towards a centralized command-and-control model and diluted the effectiveness of its leaders. De Refuge's experience was gained at a time when, for example, the position of *intendant* he occupied in Lyon was rare in France and was awarded largely on merit, and senior executives of the crown had sweeping powers and considerable latitude to act within the general guidelines set by the center. The organizational context in which De Refuge had to operate had not yet hardened into a systematized bureaucracy and relied considerably on individual initiative and persuasion. Senior positions such as he occupied enjoyed great authority, largely unchecked except by two or three top ministers and the king or regent. On one hand, we can recognize a certain anachronistic black-and-white starkness in the world he describes: a world of friends and enemies, favour and disfavour, life and death. On the other hand, though, De Refuge describes an organizational world in which we can easily relate to the ambitions and characters of the players and can easily see the modern applicability of much of his advice.

In all, Eustache de Refuge shone in the service of an increasingly organized and business-like French state. While his family connections and education certainly opened doors for him, he clearly held his higher offices on merit, and his career provided the rich experience in organizational behaviour that is evidenced in the *Treatise on the Court*. His partial or complete authorship of the *Treatise on Justice* (*Traité de la justice*) suggests a further interest in structures and governance, and his *Universal Geography* (*Geographie universelle et particulière avec un traité de la préséance du roy de France contre celuy d'Espagne*)[17] shows his keen interest in politics and the world as it was then known. The "noble and learned juriconsull and Counceller of Estate"[18] was a pioneer in a fledgling and complex structure for the management of France, a pre-bureaucratic organization marked by strong leaders and rival factions. Management was personal, life precarious, and promotion a matter of skill and ability, not entirely unlike many twenty-first century environments.

A Best-seller

The success of the practical and pragmatic *Treatise on the Court, or the Education of Courtiers* should not come as a surprise. The relative stability of national boundaries, the growth in population, the hunger for education and the development of national administrative organizations across Europe made for a receptive audience. Even Armand du Plessis, later the Duc de Richelieu, one of the greatest organization builders, is believed to have penned a number of reminders to himself[19] about how to succeed in a court environment before presenting himself to Louis XIII.

The popularity of De Refuge's work is made clear by the number of different editions, translations and variations[20] that appeared during the century or so following its first publication. We can trace at least

- Sixteen editions of the original French
- Two English translations of both books
- Two English translations of Book Two only, including *Arcana Aulica*,[21] which appeared in at least two editions; and two subsequent publications in English under different titles
- Two French translations of the second English translation (*Arcana Aulica*) of Book Two
- One Italian translation of both books
- Three editions of a Latin translation of Book Two
- Two German translations of both books
- One Dutch translation

Whatever else may be said of the *Treatise on the Court*, it was, with over forty-five known printings in six languages, a vastly popular work across Europe: an endorsement of the quality of the management and career counsel it provides.

THE *TREATISE* AS A MANAGEMENT BOOK

Eustache de Refuge's two books (particularly the second) were written and presented at the time as professional management books for the education of courtiers. While drawing on themes

A BEST SELLER

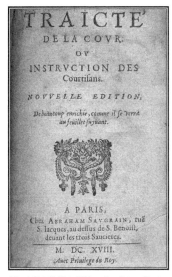

The 1618 "official" French edition. Paris, Abraham Saugrain

The 1621 Italian edition, translated by Girolamo Canini. Venice, Battista Ciotti

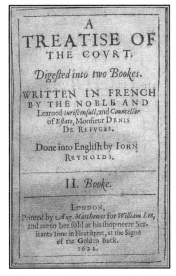

The 1622 English edition, translated by John Reynolds. London, William Lee

The 1642 Latin edition, translated by Pastorius. Amsterdam, Elzevir

A BEST SELLER

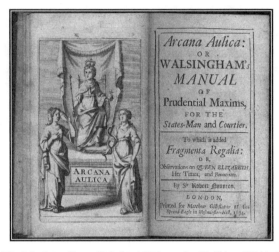

The 1694 English edition (first published in 1652), translated by Edward Walsingham. London, Matthew Gillyflower

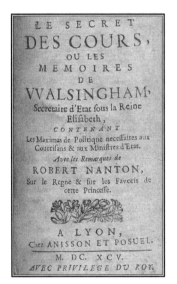

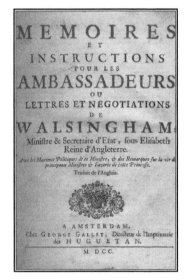

A 1695 French translation of Walsingham's 1652 translation from the French. Lyon, Anisson and Posuel

The 1700 French translation by Louis Boulesteis de la Contie of Walsingham's 1652 translation from the French. Amsterdam, Huguetan

developed during the previous century,[22] the *Treatise on the Court* is unique in its approach.

The subject matter covers the ground typically studied today in courses on management and organizational behaviour,[23] including managing people and behaviour, understanding style and attitude, motivation, self-management, conflict management, organizational power and politics, ethical problem solving, and the like. It contains probably the first treatment in a book dedicated to organizational behaviour of personality styles,[24] and an early segmentation of organizational relationships based on the intersection of position power and personal power.[25] The *Treatise* doubles as a career-counselling and coaching manual, addressing such topics as setting realistic goals, dealing with bothersome issues and dilemmas, mastering the corporate chessboard and providing recipes for action where the reader might otherwise have been stuck or ineffective. Finally, it covers ground familiar to practitioners of organizational development (for example, the challenge of working for the successor of a CEO-client), and is, of course, a self-help guide to organizational success.

De Refuge is meticulous in his categorization of individuals and groups and the logic of his presentation. He supports his various points with historical case studies and references. As an earlier translator put it, "[T]o show that his advice is not based on the vain appearances of speculation and fantasy, he backs up all his counsel with the most relevant and most celebrated authorities that history or experience can provide. By this means he adds the useful to the interesting, enables the spirit to understand the context of the facts he puts forward, and thus supports the maxims he establishes."[26] These treatments are other precursors of the modern management book genre.

SEVENTEENTH AND EIGHTEENTH
CENTURY PRESENTATION

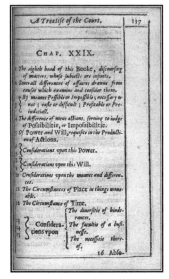

Section title, numbered chapter headings and paragraph titles. English edition, London, 1622

Numbered paragraphs. French edition, Paris, 1618

Margin notes. French edition, Cologne, 1703

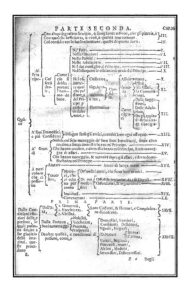

Logic diagram. Italian edition, Venice, 1621

The original presentations of the text support the classification of the *Treatise on the Court* as a management book. Most editions are divided into sections (*chefs*), numbered chapters and numbered paragraphs, with paragraph titles listed at the beginning of each chapter, supporting margin- or endnote references to sources, a subject index, a bibliography, and even (in the Italian edition)[27] a fold-out logic diagram. While such treatment was not unique at the time, it reinforces the idea that the *Treatise* was intended to be an easy-to-read reference manual.

All of this represents a considerable achievement for an author with few if any models to guide him. The *Treatise on the Court* qualifies as the first serious work on organizational behaviour and places Eustache de Refuge far ahead of his time as perhaps the first European management guru.[28] Obviously the then management context was very different from today's, but as the continuing relevance of much of De Refuge's counsel demonstrates, human nature has not changed. It's striking how his advice in the *Treatise* on topics as diverse as how to categorize management behaviours, how to respond when asked to commit illegal acts or how to use flattery resonates across some fifteen generations to appear both fresh and relevant today.

This Translation

This is a complete translation of Book Two of the 1618 "official" Paris edition[29] with royal privilege. As to the translation as a whole, I can't do better than repeat the comment of a chance acquaintance on a flight to Montreal from Miami: she, a fellow translator, introduced me to the adage that a translation is like a woman—if faithful, it may not always be interesting, if interesting, it may not always be faithful. I have tried to strike the right balance and convey Eustache de Refuge's incisive analysis and clean and yet expressive prose.

I wanted to ensure that a popular management book written in the early seventeenth century by a recently retired senior executive should appear as such to the twenty-first century reader. This has required only minor adaptations of the original.

In the case of the text, I have converted those passages addressing advice to the reader from the formal third person ("courtiers should") to the modern second person ("you should"), retaining the third person for illustrations and examples.

In the case of the presentation, I have converted the seventeenth-century genre to a modern management setting. This includes the use of point form (with no modifications to the text) where appropriate and presentation of most of the historical case studies inset and in a slightly smaller font for selective reading.

I have also converted the section titles, chapter headings and subheadings that divide the text into a modern idiom. The original exhaustive referencing and numbering and extensive paragraph headings in recital at the beginning of each chapter are very cumbersome by twenty-first century popular book standards. These were almost certainly not the work of De Refuge, but of the editor of the 1618 Paris edition.[30] So while I have broadly followed the major breaks in the original, I have reduced and shortened the headings to make them less intrusive.

I have omitted altogether the original source references, with their frequent excerpts in Latin and ancient Greek, which appeared as margin- or endnotes in most editions: I doubt they would be of much interest to management students today.[31] On the other hand, I have included a list of sources and an index as in the original. I have included some endnotes for management readers who may be interested in the historical elements and for historians who may be interested in the managerial elements: these primarily relate to sources with respect to this introduction.

CONCLUSION

The *Treatise on the Court, or the Education of Courtiers* was written at a time far removed from our own but is a treatise on an organizational context with familiar features. Its author, Eustache de Refuge, was writing from the experience of a brilliant career, making good use of his analytical talent and obvious dedication to case-study research. His work is a precursor of many modern management disciplines and offers insights that travel across four hundred years as novel, relevant and refreshing. It is remarkable both for its innovation in content and approach and for the perenniality of its ideas. It is also, I hope, fun to read.

CHRONOLOGY

LIFE AND TIMES OF EUSTACHE DE REFUGE

1559   Henri II died of a wound received jousting. He was
        succeeded by the 16-year-old Francois II, husband of
        the future Mary, Queen of Scots, with Catherine de
        Medici acting as regent.

1560   Francois II died, succeeded by his brother Charles IX.

1561   Calvin died in Geneva.

1564   **Eustache de Refuge born to a noble Parisian family
        of ancient Breton origin. His father was a member of
        the Parlements of Brittany and Paris, his mother the
        daughter of a member of the Parlement of Paris.**

1565   St. Augustine, Florida, settled by Spain.

1572   The St. Bartholomew's Day massacre (of Protestants
        by Catholics), the culmination of a decade of domestic
        wars of religion in France.

1586   **De Refuge graduated in law from the University of
        Bourges, considered the top school of its day.**

1588   Henri de Guise, Catholic claimant to the throne,
        assassinated on the orders of Henri III.

1589   Henri III assassinated, succeeded by the (then
        Protestant) King Henri of Navarre, Henri IV of
        France.

1592   Acquired a position as *conseiller* of the Parlement of Paris as part of the loyalist majority supporting Henri IV, who sat in Tours in opposition to the Catholic Duke of Guise's rump parlement in Paris.

1593   Henri IV converted to Catholicism. A period of relative internal peace ensued, lasting until Henri's assassination in 1610.

1594   Aged 35, married Helène de Bellièvre, widowed daughter of Pomponne de Bellièvre, former representative of the king in Lyon, but at this time living quietly without an official position.

1597   Dispatched by the Crown as *commissaire* to report on financial irregularities in Montpelier.

1598   Edict of Nantes regularized the position of Protestants in France.

1598/9   Pomponne de Bellièvre recalled from retirement and made chancellor of France by Henri IV.

1599   On return from Montpelier, sent to Guyenne to see to the implementation of the Edict of Nantes, then on the king's business to the Lyonnais, Dauphiné and Provence.

         Lost his bid to become lieutenant general of Toulouse to a young man "who had the great merit of contributing 7000–8000 écus" to secure the position *(Traité de la justice, in P.J.S. Dufey, Harangues de Michel L'Hospital, Chancelier de France, Paris: Auguste Boulland et Cie, 1825).*

1600   Made *maître des requêtes*, a senior position charged with the investigation and preparation of cases coming before the Parlement and providing access in the king's name to all officials and official bodies in France. It was an acknowledged stepping stone to promotion in the executive hierarchy.

1600   Henri IV at war with Savoy.

1601   Promoted by the king during his visit to Lyon to the position of intendant at Lyon. As the king's personal representative to the region, the intendant's role was one of considerable power and responsibility, Lyon being the second city of France, gateway to Savoy, the Alps and Italy, and a center of the French banking industry. De Refuge's mandate was focused primarily on improving local finances, maintaining law and order, reinforcing city defenses and seeing to the application of the Treaty of Lyon between France and Savoy.

1601   Treaty of Lyon concluded the war with Savoy, France gains Bresse, Bugey, Valromey and the Pays de Gex, contiguous to Lyon.

        Henri IV welcomed his new queen, Marie de Medici, to France at Lyon, with great pomp and celebration.

1603   Death of Queen Elizabeth I of England. She was succeeded by James VI of Scotland, James I of England.

1607   **Appointed France's ambassador to the 13 Cantons (Switzerland) at Solothurn. Required to renegotiate the alliance with the Swiss cantons, including the provision of mercenary troops for the anticipated war with the House of Austria.**

1607   Jamestown, Virginia, colony settled after earlier English attempts to settle the east coast of America had failed.

        Death of Pomponne de Bellièvre in office as chancellor of France and president of the king's council.

1608   Samuel de Champlain founded L'Acadie (Nova Scotia) and Quebec.

1610   **Raised six thousand mercenary troops for France.**

1610   Henri IV assassinated, succeeded by his wife Marie de Medici as regent for their nine-year-old son, Louis XIII.

1611   **Fled Solothurn for Colombier, Coppet then the Pays de Gex ahead of the plague.**

c. 1611   **Appointed counsellor of state.**

1611	Dispatched as ambassador to Holland, at that time maintaining an uneasy truce with Hapsburg Spain after declaring independence in 1581.
1613	Sent as ambassador to Spanish Flanders (modern-day Belgium), ruled by the Spanish Hapsburgs.
1614	**Returned as ambassador to Holland.** **Ambassador to Germany.**
1614	Revolt of the French nobility in opposition to the rule of Marie de Medici.
1615	**Appointed intendant to the army of Marshall Boisdauphin.** **Around this time, he probably wrote his *Universal Geography* and, in whole or in part, his *Treatise on Justice*.** **Probable first publication of the *Treatise on the Court, or the Education of Courtiers*, in French in Holland**
1616	Bishop Richelieu appointed secretary of state.
1616	**Appointed intendant charged with setting up a Parlement in Béarn.**
1617	Concini, favourite of Marie de Medici, assassinated on the orders of Louis XIII.
1617	**Died at age 53, leaving 6 children and a substantial fortune. Also left a magnificent library of over 1000 books on many topics, particularly geography and history.**
1620	Pilgrims settled in New England.
1624	Cardinal Richelieu made Louis XIII's chief minister.

THE AUTHOR'S
INTRODUCTION

Eustache de Refuge's introduction to the *Treatise on the Court, or the Education of Courtiers* appears as the first chapter of Book One and is particularly eloquent in its metaphors for why one should study organizational behaviour. His opening reads as follows.

> *"Getting Ahead at Court*
>
> Nowhere will you encounter interpersonal exchanges more confused or more generally difficult and thorny than at court.
>
> Usually no one throws himself into this environment unless driven by career ambition or a desire to get rich, and such passions, being anyway violent in nature, become more so in those who decide to lead such a punishing life. Furthermore, the fact that there are so many people chasing the same objective makes their initiatives

that much more violent and their behaviour that much more brusque and combative, and when restraint is called for, their dissimulation is more secretive and their tricks more malicious. Since they have to tangle with the pride and vanity of the prince's favourites (whose generally unreasonable demands they are most often unable to meet), they face personal ruin more often than personal success.

The variations of behaviour that this situation gives rise to are such that it's impossible to prescribe any hard-and-fast rules for success. In fact the best things to do will occur to you in the heat of the moment: you will make war by instinct or, as the saying goes, by eye. This wide variety of possibilities has led many to conclude that their career at court will be more marked by hazards and obstacles than by safe passages to success.

Luck and Application

The Emperor Sigismond once told one of his courtiers (who was complaining about his lack of compensation for several years of service) that often the lack of reward lay not with the unwillingness of a prince to provide one but with the ill fortune of the courtier. To illustrate his point, the emperor put two closed boxes before his follower, one filled with lead and the other with gold, and offered him one of the two as his reward. When the courtier chose the box of lead (mistakenly believing it to be the box of gold), he got the point, and while repeatedly lamenting his bad luck, didn't blame his emperor for any lack of generosity.

Of course not everything happens at court by chance. Think of it as playing a game like *primero*,[32] where the outcome is determined by a mix of skill and luck. A good player can't avoid losing when luck runs against him but will know how to capitalize when his luck is good. I might add that this is as true of life in general as it is of life at court.

The court is a theatre, an elevated stage in full view of everyone, so the twists of fate that occur there are more noticeable. But it's important not to neglect the most basic and universal rules of behaviour, even though these may not always produce the results you had hoped for. Many good pilots have been lost at sea despite their knowledge and experience of navigation, whereas others less knowledgeable, with neither astrolabe nor compass, have successfully completed many a long and perilous voyage. But none of us conclude from this that we should simply throw ourselves to the mercy of the winds without skill, science or compass.

My Limitations

I admit I'd rather you'd chosen a pilot with more knowledge than I of navigating this particular courtly sea. In my current solitude, I fear I can only sketch you a rather vague and uncertain chart and draw there the courses that the stories and examples from my recent readings of history (which my solitude now permits) have shown me. I could have used modern examples to better effect, but if one can't speak well of the living, it's altogether less dangerous not to speak of them at all. Besides, I'm sure you don't need me to tell the stories of recent situations that you know better than I.

The Structure of the Two Books

To inject an element of organization into such a confused subject, I will address first the competences that I believe to be most requisite in a courtier and then how you may apply these, be they

- to advance in favour,
- to maintain yourself in favour, or
- to anticipate your fall so that this may be as gentle and as honourable as possible."

Book One

As outlined in the author's introduction and elsewhere, the major part of Book One addresses the competences needed for a successful career at court, and Book Two addresses how to put these into practise in the day-to-day organizational world.

Book One therefore provides an important backdrop to Book Two, and the key points it makes, if more philosophical than practical, are intended to condition the reader to apply the generic approaches suggested. A summary of its principal themes appears in the following box.

TREATISE ON THE COURT: BOOK ONE

"Wherein is very amply set forth the principal parts requisite and necessary in a courtier."

The first book of the *Treatise on the Court, or the Education of Courtiers* concerns itself with the personal qualities and social skills required of anyone hoping to achieve success and promotion at court. It is roughly the same length as Book Two and addresses subjects as diverse as style of dress, personality types and the various distractions that can mar perceptionss of good and evil.

De Refuge divides Book One into eight sections (*chefs*), each of which tackles a different skill or attribute that a courtier must consider if he or she is to pursue a successful career.

The major themes are as follows:

1. Being affable and well-liked.

2. Using good judgment, and noting the things that impair judgment.

3. Identifying perceptions of good and evil that motivate our actions and how to influence these perceptions in others.

4. Judging what's good and what's evil and the things that can prevent us from exercising good judgment.

5. Adapting our behaviour to suit the style or character of others, with an outline of the most common personality traits.

6. Understanding how age and fortune can alter personality.

7. Using the above knowledge to enable project success.

8. Speaking graciously and effectively, and dealing with those who don't.

Above all, De Refuge urges the reader to closely observe the people he interacts with, and then to take appropriate steps to make himself pleasant and respectable to the broad cross-section he will inevitably encounter.

In short, he provides a generic framework for organizing thinking and proposes that the career courtier tailor his style and tactics to his specific situation, thereby maximizing his chances of success.

Book One ends with this introduction to Book Two:

"So much for the attributes that are most necessary in a courtier. Let us look now at how you should apply these daily."

TREATISE
ON
THE COURT

or the Education of Courtiers

BOOK TWO

GAINING ACCESS
AND RECOGNITION

MOTIVATIONS AT COURT

In life, our actions should always be driven by our principal goals, and the goals of those who throw themselves at the court are very diverse. Some hunger for power, and a few (according to Seneca) want to mistreat, hinder and bully others; very few actually go to court to serve and help advance the business of their prince.

ACCESS AND RECOGNITION[33]

Whatever their goals may be, everyone who goes to court shares the common objective of gaining their prince's favour. To this end they apply all their skill and effort.

In this regard, there are two preconditions to princely favour:

- that he knows the person seeking his favour, and
- that he recognizes the value of this person's actions, behaviour or other attributes.

ACCESS

Some people have automatic access to the prince, typically because of their families' status or the authority and responsibility of some office they personally hold. This applies whether the position they occupy is important or not and whether it was inherited or simply purchased. These people don't have to invest in making themselves known to the prince: they are almost half-way home.[34]

Those Without Access

Less fortunate courtiers find the first part of the task, becoming known to the prince, far more difficult. But once they succeed, assuming the prince considers them qualified, they often rise above the others. Because they have been promoted from poor or humble beginnings (though sometimes already from the nobility), they are generally more submissive, obedient and respectful of the will of the prince who raised them up. They acknowledge him as the father of their good fortune and are, to use a courtly expression, his creations.

Those With Access

Those who are born great and have automatic access to the prince don't behave this way. The status of their family or their own public office can lead them to put their own honour or objectives ahead of those of their prince. The prince, in turn, is often jealous of them and may be unwilling to promote them for fear that they will criticize or control him if he gives them too much power, and that he might not be able to demote them later without danger to both his person and his kingdom.

On the other hand, it's far easier for the prince to demote someone of more humble origins. All he has to do is turn his back on him and abandon him to the resentment of more powerful colleagues.

The above only applies to princes who have the wisdom to place reasonable limits on the power of the favourites they promote. Some princes have tried conferring all of their kingdom's high honours and riches on just one person and requiring the great nobles to report to him, but this has nearly always ended badly.

RECOGNITION

Of the various avenues that have been used by courtiers seeking to advance in recognition and authority, two have been more often traveled than the rest.

Work Your Way Up

The first method is to go after commissions, public offices, and titles and climb the stairs of recognition step by step until you come close to the prince himself.

Perform Confidential Tasks

The second is for you to follow the court and look for opportunities to be entrusted with special mandates and personal commissions by your prince.

This second avenue is certainly the quickest route to favour and has been taken by those who have gained the utmost favour of their princes.

> Maecenas endeared himself to Augustus in this way, and Sallust used the technique with Augustus and for a while with his successor, Tiberius.

> Tacitus says that Seneca's brother Mella, to become as powerful as a consul with a minimum of delay, turned his back on the pursuit of high offices and titles in favour of carrying out tasks and private commissions for the emperor himself.

BECOMING KNOWN

There are also various ways to make yourself known to your prince and to get him to appreciate you. These vary depending on the situation and its context.

Sometimes people can get themselves noticed through a high-profile service or action, or thanks to some unusual personal quality or aptitude. Otherwise, third-party recommendations are the most frequently used way to get introduced to and noticed by a prince.

GET AN INTRODUCTION

Princes live in a world so far above others and are hemmed in by such a crowd of lords and veteran courtiers that it's hard for a newcomer to be noticed unless someone who is already established takes him by the hand and makes room for him to approach.

DO SOMETHING EXTRAORDINARY

The exception to the need to be introduced is the person who manages unaided to do something so extraordinary that everyone notices him, including the prince.

> The story is told of the architect Deinocrates (otherwise known as Stasicrates), who wanted to attract the attention of Alexander the Great. After every courtier had refused to introduce him, he came up with the idea of appearing to Alexander stark naked, covered in oil, with a crown of poplar branches on his head, a lion skin over his left shoulder and a great club in his right hand. Thus dressed, he sought out Alexander while he was dispensing justice from his throne, and the novelty of the spectacle grabbed the attention of everyone present. Alexander had him brought forward, and (though he did not endorse his behaviour) after giving Deinocrates an audience, had him enrolled in his entourage.

I don't quote this example to encourage you to make such a theatrical entrance to get noticed, but rather to show that if you're unknown you will be hard-pressed to break through the kind of crowd that surrounds a prince unless you're assisted by someone who already has access. Your alternative is to stage some unusual act or to benefit from some chance encounter that will get you noticed.

WINNING YOUR
PRINCE'S FAVOUR

KNOWING WHO YOU'RE DEALING WITH

If you're a courtier who wants to be known to and loved by his prince, you must carefully observe not only his behaviour but also that of

- his most trusted servants,
- the great nobles in his entourage, and
- anyone else who might help you.

Take care to identify as well anyone who might work against you, be it for reasons of jealousy, fear, envy or hate, or because of their own or their friends' self-interest.

PRINCELY INCLINATIONS

You should observe the disposition of your prince, which will usually reflect his temperament.

Wise princes often try to disguise what they're thinking, but it's hard for them to do this well enough not to be found out; their actions are all so public that it's relatively easy to judge which way they lean. In fact, sometimes they are so stung by the weight of business that they have no choice but to reveal the true workings of their minds. Even Tiberius, the most cunning and secretive prince of all, could not play his role well enough to prevent all his contemporaries from seeing through him and understanding his true nature.

A prince's inclinations (like any man's) are diverse and almost infinite, but they can generally be condensed into two main categories:

- the first comprises everything that concerns the greatness of the state he rules;
- the second, everything that concerns his personal pleasures.

Greatness

The greatness of a prince's state comprises, depending on the prince in question,

- his reputation,
- his wealth,
- the obedience of his subjects, or
- the valour and faithfulness of his armies.

When such matters are at stake, you need to understand the realities facing your prince and what he's trying to achieve. The advisors he considers best equipped to help him reach his ends, provided they are neither suspect nor unwelcome for other reasons, will be the ones most welcome at his side.

Personal Pleasures

You should approach your prince's hedonistic pleasures and corrupt inclinations in much the same way. If, like Tiberius, he's a mistrustful and fearful person, he'll value an aggressive and self-assured assistant who's ready to do his bidding and isn't afraid of offending the powerful people around him. These are the qualities that Tacitus describes in Sejanus.

If your prince is enjoying an episode of drunken debauchery, he will want to be surrounded by other drinkers.

Tiberius loved the company of Pomponius Flaccus and Lucius Piso for this reason and would sometimes spend two whole days and a night drinking with them, referring to them as his friends in everything, twenty-four hours a day. One he rewarded with the province of Syria, the other with the prefecture of the city of Rome.

This same emperor chose a little-known man of low standing over many noble candidates for quaestor because, it is said, the man had downed the contents of a 96-glass jar of wine.

Nero's lasciviousness led him to favour Tigellinus, who helped him assuage his lust; it also led him to keep C. Petronius close to him to evaluate the degree of elegance of his various excesses.

Commodus and Heliogaballus awarded all of their empire's highest offices to men who were as corrupt as they.

Vespasian didn't love and value Mucianus for his fidelity or behaviour but rather because he fed his avarice.

After the death of Theodorus Castamonita, his uncle Isacus Angelus, the emperor of Constantinople, promoted a young clerk of the treasury. The clerk hardly knew how to write, but Isacus Angelus raised him to a position of authority simply to get a share of the bribes and gifts that the boy could extract from the people who used his services.

The emperor Manuel Comnenus wanted a determined tax collector who would be capable of raising all kinds of new taxes without the people realizing what he was doing. In this way, he hoped to increase his income enough to pay for his extravagant spending. According to Nicetas, he chose John of Putzé, a crude and choleric man who was insufferable and hard to approach: just the kind of man normally appointed to this sort of job. On top of this, the emperor gave Putzé so much authority that he usurped the functions of all the other ministers and even the authority to contradict the edicts of his prince and the Senate. In the name of economy, this Putzé slashed some of the state's most essential expenditures, including the maintenance of the galleys, the principal military force of the empire.

SUPPORTING YOUR PRINCE

We don't need more examples to establish the maxim, well-known and too often practised by those who spend time with princes, that anyone who wants to be accepted by his prince must find a way to support him in his inclinations and passions.

PERSONAL INTEGRITY

The inclinations of princes so often fall outside the bounds of all reason and prudence that men of integrity can be forgiven for believing that aiding them will inevitably lead to their downfall at court.

However, it must be said that the court is a great whore who sooner or later corrupts even the most virtuous and chaste of men. In truth, anyone who aspires to live a life of innocence far from the daily existence of most men (who are lacking in many ways and are prey to their own passions) would do well to avoid it.

As evidence of this, you'd do well to reflect on a few examples of courtly corruption.

> Festinus, a friend of Maximinus, governed Asia during Valentinian's reign with great kindness and class. He was originally a sharp critic of Maximinus' cruelty and the slander he used to get his way but eventually realized that it was this behaviour that had earned Maximinus authority over the praetorian bands, making him second only to the emperor himself in importance. So Festinus decided to change his ways and thereafter committed many cruelties and injustices.

> Consider also John of Putzé (who I've already mentioned), who initially managed Emperor Manuel's business and treasury with great integrity, making the emperor's pride and brutality more tolerable. But eventually, according to Nicetas, he resolved to enrich himself as had

his predecessors and invited his friends to do the same. This they did, and even those who were more honest and less corrupt were obliged to conform for fear that they would suffer if they tried to stop him.

Arastides, "the Just" in name and deed, was appointed treasurer of Athens. At the beginning of his term, he wanted to behave honourably and prevent his subordinates from robbing the treasury. He was at once charged with being the biggest thief of all time and one of the most corrupt men ever to hold his office. He narrowly escaped a sentence of death, and when he was finally acquitted and resumed his position, he decided to imitate his predecessors, turning a blind eye to the customary theft of his companions. In this way, he quickly regained his public reputation.

Such things happen in the courts of most princes either through the malice of people in high government positions (who can't abide anyone more virtuous than themselves) or through the negligence and stupidity of princes themselves.

The Role of Good Men

It is difficult for good men to remain honest for long in such an environment. In spite of this, they may be drawn to this kind of life

- out of personal necessity,
- to uphold their family names,
- because their office demands it,
- because they are summoned by their prince, or
- because they want to serve their country or their friends.

As an honourable man, you can, in my opinion, retain your integrity, at least for a while. And depending on what fate holds in store, you can hope to benefit both yourself and others.

In all of this, I'm speaking of the courts of the worst princes, for to live in the court of a wise and knowledgeable prince is much less difficult.

A Force for Good

Good men are often advised to take up public office not only for the good of their country but also to keep bad men out of power. I believe that good men should try to get close to a tyrant or a voluptuous prince for the same reason. From that position, they are best able, if not directly and openly then at least indirectly or surreptitiously, to impede that prince's evil and pernicious inclinations by

- orchestrating delays,
- throwing obstacles in his way, or
- proposing milder and more plausible solutions.

> Burrus and Seneca were two wise courtiers who were considered in their day to be most honest and virtuous. When ordered to train the young Nero, they recognized that his naturally bad character could never really be altered. He was strongly inclined to lasciviousness and was about to sleep with several married women and cause scandals among the families of Rome, so Burrus and Seneca resolved to quench his lust and desire by procuring him a mistress, who kept his youthful ardour in check for a while. They covered up the affair with the pretense that a friend of Seneca's, Annaeus Serenus, was in fact the woman's lover, and Nero gave her gifts in this man's name.

In this way, if an honest man is unable to deter a prince's debauchery, excesses or evil designs, he should quietly divert these tendencies towards ends that are less harmful to others and to the honour of the prince.

Some say that a tyrant or a dissolute prince seldom listens to an honest man. I admit that this is certainly rare, but few courts are so destitute that there are no good men present at all. If these people haven't been called there by the prince, then they're there out of a desire to do good for others and to counterbalance the power of evil men. They enlist the support of the least bad of the others or are linked to some powerful patron by ties of affection, familiarity or common interest. They manage to hold their positions by avoiding speaking out against the violent inclinations of their prince but not allowing themselves to slip into vile and abject servitude by participating in his wicked or tyrannical schemes.

> You should imitate the behaviour of Lepidus under Tiberius, who Tacitus set up as an example of a good and wise courtier. Tacitus also commended Capito, who had discretely maintained his liberty at court and had been privy to everything, and Labeo, who had earned the prince's favour through obedience.

Honesty Pays

I don't deny that an honest man will find life as a courtier far harder than will an evil one, but he will at least enjoy more honour and inner peace.

If a good man behaves wisely and doesn't confront his prince over what he can't make him change, I assure you that even the worst prince will value and favour him more than he will his dishonest rivals. Among bad men, it is rare to find the faithfulness needed to serve a master that one can hope to find in a good man.

> It was the advice of Sallust to Julius Caesar, and of Mycenas to Augustus, to employ mainly good men because their honour and conscientious regard for duty restrains them more effectively than the fear of punishment or their lack of ability can bridle the ambitions of bad men.

The Role of Bad Men

As I have said, there are always many more bad men than good at court, and they're typically useful to bad princes in one of two ways.

- The first is that they flatter their princes and carry out their evil plans, their obedience enhanced by the approval and applause they receive for their behaviour.
- The second is that they enable princes to seem better than they are in contrast to the bad men who surround them, which makes some princes feel more secure in their company.

> When Dionysius, the tyrant of Syracuse, was asked to expel a close advisor who was universally hated, he refused on the grounds that if he expelled him, he would himself become the most hated person at his own court.

It's customary for anyone who knows that he's prone to a particular vice to try to appear less bad by setting himself in comparison with others who are even worse. This is the origin of a common courtly trick: choosing an unpromising successor so that one's own actions can appear better and more illustrious by comparison.

> They say this is why Augustus took Tiberius as his successor, and likewise why Tiberius left the empire to Caligula.

Be Brief

A good man should, above all, be brief and reserved when he speaks; bad princes seldom appreciate any man of honour speaking freely to them.

Plato ended up badly after speaking too liberally to Dionysius of Syracuse: he was handed over to a ship's captain to be sold into slavery in Crete. The group of philosophers who ransomed him warned him to either abstain entirely from the company of princes or to learn to please them.

Aristotle gave similar counsel to his relative Callisthenes who was at the court of Alexander, advising that he should speak only rarely and then only of things that would please the man who held the power of life and death over him.

USING FLATTERY

There's no way you can avoid using at least some flattery to get into the good graces of your prince. You must take care, though, because not any kind of flattery will suffice. The base and humble sort of flattery displeased even Tiberius, who frequently complained on leaving the Senate of the cowardly and servile behaviour of the senators.

FLATTER WISELY

Sometimes flattery can do you more harm than good. If you flatter someone too much, he'll suspect that you're planning to betray him. There must be (say Eschines and Plutarch) a real point and a semblance of independent thought mixed in with the flattery if you expect to convince your prince (or anyone for that matter) that you're sincere. This is the way to maintain your credibility.

> When Croesus was king, he showed how well versed he was in the appetites of kings and what would please or displease them. Cambyses, king of the Persians, once asked his entourage how they felt he compared to his father Cyrus. Everyone told him he was a far

greater king than Cyrus because he'd expanded his father's kingdom by the addition of Egypt and control of the seas. When Croesus came to speak, though, he affirmed that Cambyses was far inferior to his father Cyrus because he didn't yet have a son who was his equal. This answer (says Herodotus) satisfied the vanity of this prince more than the others because it appeared to be more honest.

Volarius Messala was the first to use this type of "honest" flattery with Tiberius, proposing that the oath of allegiance to Tiberius should be renewed every year. When Tiberius suddenly asked him whether he, Tiberius, had ordered him to make that recommendation, Messala answered that on the contrary, he was acting of his own accord. He said that in matters of state he would take no man's advice but his own and would say what he thought regardless of who might be offended by it. Of all the kinds of flattery, says Tacitus, this is the only one you should use.

Aetius Capito subsequently used a similar approach when Tiberius forbade the prosecution of Annius, a Roman gentleman accused of defiling the prince's image by using it on his silver dishes. Aetius openly opposed this order as being contrary to the freedom and authority of the Senate. He took the position that Tiberius should not take this power on himself but should leave the Senate to punish the act. He added that Tiberius was entitled to pardon offences against himself but not offences against the state.

There are other examples, but these will serve to demonstrate that if you must resort to flattery, you should be careful that it will not occasion any public or private harm. Use it only to satisfy the prince's vanity.

ADVISING YOUR PRINCE

You must also be wary not to counsel a haughty prince, even if asked, if you can avoid it.

Consider the example of Xerxes' decision to invade Greece. At that time, he summoned the princes of Asia, saying he wanted to consult with them. Once they arrived, though, he told them he'd called a meeting in council to avoid the appearance of acting alone without their advice but that he expected no opposition and no debate.

When Cambyses, ruler of the Persians before Xerxes, decided to marry his sister, he asked his council whether any law of Persia prohibited a king from marrying his sister. His council realized that their prince was not trying to decide what to do but wanted to find out if they approved of the marriage, so they responded that though there was no law specifically permitting it, there was a law that provided that a king could do no wrong.

If a prince appears to be asking for your input on something, weigh both his humour and the nature of the affair before responding.

In our fathers' time, a prince less exalted than a king, but nevertheless viceroy of Spain, advised the greatest nobles of that country that they weren't expected to challenge what was put to them in the councils and assemblies of state. When King Ferdinand died, the pope and the emperor Maximilian advised Charles of Austria (who was in Flanders at the time) to assume the Crown of Spain even though his mother Joan, Ferdinand's daughter, was still alive but in poor health and unfit to govern. The notables of the realm were assembled for their approval, and Cardinal Jimenez laid out the justification for this manoeuvre. The nobles objected openly, more observant of ancient custom and of honouring their queen than of being good followers to he who would inherit the kingdom when she was gone. This angered Jimenez, and he rose and told them that the matter was not to be called into question and that he didn't need their advice because a king didn't need the authorization of his subjects to act within his realm. He'd brought them together for their own good and advantage, of which he had always been mindful, so that by approving this appointment they could endear themselves to their new prince. But since they'd given themselves as a right what they had been asked as a courtesy, he, Jimenez, would have Charles immediately proclaimed king in Madrid so that the other towns would follow this example.

Help Him Decide

Princes act haughtily like this most of the time and not only on occasions like those listed above. They seldom ask for advice unless they want approval for something they've already decided to do or to probe the willingness of those they pretend to consult: this is how Tiberius usually treated the Roman Senate.

As a courtier, you should therefore strive to read your prince's mind and avoid giving advice that might be badly received. When you've guessed his real intentions, you should appear to analyze the matter and lay out the pros and cons. Then, if possible, leave the prince to make his own decision. Unless he's already firmly resolved, a prince will readily change his mind once he understands the potential flaws in his stratagem.

Great men are often reluctant to change their minds because they fear this will make them seem inferior to their advisors, but if you avoid proposing a specific alternative, you can avoid having your prince restrained by fear of such an embarrassment. Furthermore, an advisor will certainly be blamed for his advice if this leads to an outcome unwelcome to the prince.

If the prince does pursue his original idea and it doesn't work out, he'll think well of the counsellor who anticipated the problems that could have been avoided and pointed them out to him.

Illegal Acts

If you're pressed for an opinion on something illegal, you should

- either find an excuse to delay giving it, or

- recommend that another advisor be called in so the proposal can be more carefully evaluated and the decision made that will best protect the dignity and safety of your prince.

> Burrus deterred Nero's first attempt on the life of his mother by this means, promising that he'd kill her himself should the accusations against her be found to be true and insisting that Nero shouldn't condemn her before the circumstances had been fully investigated. He argued that Nero should not rush to punish his own mother more quickly than he would any other citizen, who would always be allowed to defend himself against his accusers. While the inquiry was being conducted, Nero's fury abated and his fears diminished, so through the delay, Burrus was able, on this occasion, to head off his prince's unholy resolution.

This approach, however, can't be used under just any circumstances and should be reserved for only the worst situations. Before using it, you must first weigh whether or not your prince will brook such delays; some princes are so quick to act and so impatient with delay and difficulty that those who resort to this tactic all too often fall from favour because of it.

For this reason you must try to have a rich and abundant variety of solutions to propose to some princes and not allow yourself to get caught with no initiative to suggest.

PREVENTING THE WRONG THING

When your prince consults you, it's less likely to be about what he should do than about how he can get done something that he's already decided to do.

SLOW THINGS DOWN

On occasions when you judge the proposed action to be against all reason and duty, you should recommend the slowest and most drawn-out approach you can think of. You can justify this on the grounds of ease of implementation, fairness and minimization of risk. Fast-track projects generally present major difficulties and are highly risky, which gives you what you need to oppose them.

Unless he's carried away by impatience, a prince, having no objective other than to get what he wants, will always choose the safest and most appealing expedients, even if they will take longer. In such circumstances he'll not find fault with someone who proposes a plausible but less hasty approach. He will not question the circumspection of the one who made the suggestion or his motivation to help his leader reach his goal easily and safely.

If it should happen that difficulties do result from a prince's headlong course of action, the prudence of the advisor who suggested an alternative approach will appear that much greater. And if he does adopt a more drawn-out approach, something may happen to

- cool his enthusiasm, or
- make him realize the impossibility or impracticality of what he's planning.

Don't Obstruct

Sometimes, however, you may see that your prince is determined to adopt an approach that will run into trouble from the beginning or prove impossible to carry out successfully. When this happens, you should avoid supporting his approach and instead, respectfully and without comment, let him go ahead. You're better off keeping quiet and letting him move forward: if you try to dissuade him, he may look for others who will be more amenable to carrying out his unprincipled plan, whereas he might have abandoned it if he'd been left to proceed and had run into obstacles from the outset.

ORDERS TO DO WRONG

It can happen that a prince's impatience will lead him to order an honest man to carry out some plan of his that's unethical. Responding to such a proposition can perplex the best of us, especially if the importance and nature of the affair is such that you can't find a way to

- get out of it, or
- decline the responsibility and bring in someone else to take care of it.

> Burrus employed this strategy when he wanted to deter Nero from another attempt on his mother's life. She had escaped from the "shipwreck" he had contrived for her, and fearing that this vindictive and cruel woman would never forgive him this attempted assassination, he resolved once again to do away with her. Burrus and Seneca (according to Tacitus) looked at each other long and hard before saying anything. Finally Seneca, seeing the prince's agitation, asked Burrus whether he thought the deed could be left to the soldiers of the guard. Burrus didn't want to dirty his hands or those of the soldiers, so he replied that he didn't think they'd want to kill Nero's mother given their love for the house and blood of the Caesars, from whom his mother, Agrippina, was descended. He suggested that Anicetus, who had undertaken to do the deed in the first place, should finish it, and in this way they both evaded guilt for the matricide.

I admit that it's no act of charity to leave someone else to carry out an evil task like this, but in such circumstances, I think it more fitting that someone like Anicetus do it than that an honest or virtuous man should dirty his hands with it.

The safest way to manage the unjust or illegal projects of your prince is to anticipate and deal with them

- either before they are born, or at least
- before they can become well rooted in his mind.

Persuasion

Many advisors have successfully used soft dissuasion and "silken words," as Parysatis put it. But to adopt this technique, you need to have great influence over your prince, and he must be more disposed to follow the paths of reason than his own inclinations. Unfortunately, this is a rare trait, and even if you find a prince who acts like this, he will only do so on the odd occasion: this approach is not a universal solution.

Stories

I also recommend a tactic that has been successfully adopted by nimble-witted people with a gift for storytelling. They speak familiarly to their prince without in any way diminishing the respect they show him and with great finesse will tell a tale about something vaguely similar to what he has in mind. Through the story they are able to get him to see the danger, downside and potential consequences of his plan, all indirectly, using other words and pretexts. But besides a quick wit and a skilful presentation, this approach requires that your prince not realize that you created the whole tale for him for a purpose.

Tiberius imagined that the tragedy *Atreus*, authored by Scaurus, had been written expressly to criticize him for killing his relatives.

Domitian thought that Helvidius' account of Paris and Oenone was a reproach for his divorce.

You have to be careful to weave your stories in skilfully among other subjects that don't involve or directly concern the prince's project; they must be dropped in casually and lightly at just the right moment. Only good fortune can bring the prince to see the implications of his own actions in a story you tell, and when the story appears to have been recounted innocently with no specific purpose, he'll be more receptive to its message and will benefit from it more.

OTHER OPTIONS

There are other things you can do that fall between either fruitlessly opposing or maliciously supporting your prince's evil designs. You can draw ideas from

- topics that come up in the normal course of events,
- chance happenings, or
- people who are close to the prince.

If you're obliged to go against something your prince has set his heart on, then at the same time you should voice your support for some other project of his about which he is equally passionate. Be careful to emphasize that your advice is driven by the duty and respect you owe him.

This is what Mucianus did to Domitian to keep him in the paths of duty and prevent him from joining up with Cerealis.

DEALING WITH THE FOUR
TYPES OF PRINCE

To employ any of these strategies successfully with a prince, as with any man you must first understand his particular temperament. Because they enjoy more power than the people around them, princes tend to be less in control of their passions and humours, which for the most part are more violent and less restrained by reason than those of the average person.

THE CHOLERIC TEMPERAMENT

A person of choleric character generally

- is hasty
- is haughty
- wants everyone to bend to his command
- is intolerant of any disobedience
- is impatient in the execution of all his ventures
- is overly hasty in making decisions
- doesn't ask the advice of others except to find someone to do his bidding
- is offensive
- is quick to offend others but quick to forget the offence as long as the other person appears to have forgotten it; if the other person doesn't, he becomes vindictive and nurses a lasting hatred towards him

Dealing With a Choleric Prince

When you have to deal with a person of choleric humour, you must keep your eyes and ears open. Stay on your toes and see, understand, say and do what the prince wants immediately and without complaint; if you don't, he may suspect you think you know better than he. Follow all of his instructions humbly and obediently, even if they are below your dignity. If he wrongs you, be patient and quick to forget the offence: in fact, redouble your efforts to serve him and your obedience. Try to win his gratitude and recognition through your good services, but never remind him of what you've done for him for fear that he may take this as a criticism. Be sure to avoid him entirely during the great and extreme bursts of anger to which he is prone: at such times everything displeases him, and even his closest friends can't do anything right in his eyes. Familiarity leads to contempt with choleric princes, and for this reason, you should avoid becoming too personal with them, even if encouraged to do so. Instead, always treat them with great modesty and respect.

Such princes are like lions; they can be tamed for a while, but in the end they will devour those who thought they knew them well and thought they could control them.

THE SANGUINE TEMPERAMENT

A person of sanguine character generally

- is happy
- loves pleasure, games and fun
- avoids melancholy and sadness
- avoids difficult or contentious business
- avoids quarrels
- loves peace and quiet
- gladly leaves the management of his affairs to subordinates
- dislikes being disturbed, and appreciates people who carry out his instructions in ways that don't cause disruption.
- is courteous and gracious
- dislikes hurting anyone, and if he does hurt them, it's usually with words rather than deeds
- is as willing to forget the wrongs done to him as he is the wrongs he has done to others
- enjoys making people happy
- is liberal and open-minded

Dealing With a Sanguine Prince

If you work with a sanguine prince, you must show him the respect due to him but talk about serious business as little as possible.

Even if you're managing the weightiest and most important affairs of state, you shouldn't approach a sanguine prince unless summoned, or at least not until you're sure he's not at play or indulging in a preferred pastime. Otherwise you may embarrass him by interrupting some favourite relaxation and make him feel that you secretly disapprove of these pleasures.

> Philip, King of Macedon, was playing dice when he was told that Antipater was at his door wanting to speak to him. Annoyed and angry, he threw the board and dice aside onto a bed, ashamed that Antipater might have seen him at play.

If you succeed in becoming someone who manages the greatest affairs of state, you'll have a great advantage because your prince will delegate everything to you. But you'll also have a great disadvantage because it will be difficult for you to get your prince to attend to business matters, such things being in conflict with his sanguine humour.

Courtiers who are jovial but also good business managers generally do best with such a prince, provided they maintain the gravity of their position when they aren't with him. Failing this, they will be criticized by others, and from this criticism will grow the courage to criticize them for other things. To resolve such complaints, the prince will get rid of the person who was the apparent cause of the problem.

THE MELANCHOLY TEMPERAMENT

A melancholy prince is

- slow and late to make decisions
- distracted
- distrustful
- suspicious
- ingenious
- usually malicious
- a man of few words, used mainly to probe the thinking of those who approach him
- uses language that is generally ambiguous and full of double meanings, even (as we see in Tiberius) when dealing with the thorniest issues
- secretive and a dissembler
- opinionated
- an enemy of mirth and familiarity
- retiring and solitary
- hard to approach and talk to
- few people's friend, and then only coldly
- prone to hatred on the smallest pretext because of his perpetual fear of betrayal
- covetous and fearful, sometimes to an extreme, believing that ownership of the whole earth might somehow not be enough for him
- an enemy to those he has offended as much as to those that have offended him
- vindictive and unforgiving, so that even if you manage to make up with him, you shouldn't put too much faith in the reconciliation

Dealing With a Melancholy Prince

In your relations with someone of this humour, you should keep the bridle in your hands at all times and proceed with great restraint and circumspection. Be very controlled; weigh every word that passes your lips, and say nothing that's unnecessary or may not be well received. It's safest to say nothing out of turn and to speak only when spoken to. In everything you do, act with great respect and caution towards your prince and avoid contradicting him. Don't oppose a melancholy prince when he makes a decision, or his melancholy may burst into flames of anger.

Be careful not to ask for something he might refuse. It's dangerous to let such a prince get used to saying no to you: his melancholy makes him naturally prone to suspicion, and he may come to believe that his refusal has offended you. If he feels you're upset, he'll suspect that you have become his enemy, and you'll have to work miracles to get him to change his mind. People like this never forget an offence and will assume that you don't forget an offence either.

In short, this melancholy temperament is the most desolate, difficult and unstable of all, both because of the variety and strangeness of what it conjures up in the imagination and because such people are the hardest to deal with.

THE PHLEGMATIC TEMPERAMENT

A phlegmatic prince has the heaviness and slowness of a melancholy prince but doesn't share his melancholy attitudes, malice, or fear that bad things will happen. The coldness that freezes his heart leads him to mistrust himself more than he does others. He

- is afraid to act out of fear of failure, and doesn't know how to proceed
- lacks resolve
- is hesitant in implementation
- lacks insight
- hates with little bitterness and loves with little passion

Dealing With a Phlegmatic Prince

It takes an active, courageous and inventive spirit to warm the coldness of this humour. But once a prince has realized that his advisor can fix things that he himself, given his limitations, thought unfixable, then he loves and admires this man and comes to believe he can't do without him. This sort of patronage, based on need, is often the most enduring of all. Knowing this, make it your business to find solutions to the most seemingly difficult situations from which your leader expects little or no success.

You should also work to prevent anyone more adept than yourself from coming between you and your prince, and for this reason you should avoid long absences from court. If some other person is recognized as better than you at doing something, you'll be considered less necessary, and if the prince becomes used to doing without you for a while, he may feel that he can do without you forever. I hardly need to point out that one of the most common tricks of managers at court is to recruit only assistants who are far inferior to themselves in both social status and capability. This way, their own contribution shines brighter by comparison, and they avoid the risk of being supplanted should the prince find among such assistants someone more to his taste. Furthermore, unlike their nobler or more honest counterparts, such people are capable of hurting you or covering up the corruption of their patrons at your expense.

THE INFLUENCE OF CONTEXT

These, then, are the four humours of which all men and all princes are made. Everyone inclines to one side or another, according to the degree of the humour that dominates them most.

But these humours are not fixed forever. A person's humour can change with age, with the events in his life or with the topic under discussion, and then his behaviour will change accordingly. This is as true of princes as it is of anyone else.

WAR AND PEACE

In times of war, you'll see that a prince's affection and attention will be reserved for generals and warriors. In peacetime, though, when the need has passed, he'll take little notice of them. In turning his attention to pleasures or some other passion, he'll transfer his affection to those who will be useful to him in these areas.

> Tiberius behaved one way under Augustus, another during the lives of Germanicus and Drusus, another while his mother Livia was alive, another during the time he either loved or feared Sejanus, and differently yet again once he had gotten rid of the last.

> Passenius says that there was never a better servant than Caligula during the time of Tiberius, nor a worse master than when he succeeded him as emperor.

> When Plutarch writes of how Marius and Sylla changed their ways over time, he questions whether their luck in life actually changed their basic natures or whether it simply uncovered hidden parts of their true selves.

FUNDAMENTAL NATURES

In reality, the fundamental nature of most people doesn't change, but parts of it that may have been suppressed by fear will surface publicly once that fear goes away, as Leontius said of Zenon. As the snake is to the peasant, so are such people to you: trembling with cold they cannot hurt you, but warmed by the sun they will begin to spit their venom.

> Josephus tells us that while Tryphon was leading a private life, he won over the people by seeming to be the very picture of a good and honourable man. But as soon as he was made king, he discarded his mask and showed himself for what he had always been.
>
> Euripides reproaches Agamemnon for something similar. Until he was made general of the Greeks, Agamemnon was a humble and approachable man. After his election, though, he became an enemy to his friends and stayed locked in his house and largely inaccessible. Euripides adds that a good man managing important responsibilities must never change his behaviour, but this advice is seldom (or, in fact, never) taken, except possibly by Pollion as he is described by Seneca.

THE PRIDE OF PRINCES

The worst and most common faults seen in princes are born of excessive pride, a frequent companion of power that makes it next to impossible for them to accept advice. Their pride convinces them that because they're more powerful than their subjects they are also more competent. Some even believe that they can obey neither law nor reason without surrendering part of their authority, feeling that they can't be truly sovereign if there are any limits to their power. It seems to them that they'd be no better than the common man should they restrict themselves to only those things permitted the common man. They believe that the rules of piety, honour and justice were created for ordinary people, not for them.

It would be one thing if such tyrannical delusions possessed only the spirits of ordinary princes, but it seems that power sometimes seduces even the brightest and the best.

> No one in history passed down sounder teachings on the art of moderation than the men known as the Seven Sages of Greece, yet the world has never seen worse tyrants than some of their number who ruled at that time.

> Appian, speaking of Aristo and other philosophers who had tyrannized Athens, adds that the Pythagoreans, who enjoyed a measure of power in Italy, were the most wicked tyrants of their day. All this casts doubt on whether the philosophers, when they disdained honours and high offices, really meant what they said or were just trying to rationalize their own poverty and idleness. If we believe Aristophanes, the Pythagoreans used frugality and parsimony more as ways to cope with their poverty and need than for any noble reason; they were quite happy to feast and party at someone else's expense.

THE INFLUENCE OF IMPOSTORS

The suggestions, flattery and applause of the worthless and unscrupulous impostors who most often surround princes contribute greatly to changing them. Tacitus attributes the pride and cruelty of Vitellius to this kind of charlatan, and it was this sort of advisor who taught the good-natured Vespasian to oppress his subjects and burden them with new and heavy taxes. In short, princes generally change under the influence of such counsellors.

Betrayal

Such men seek favour for themselves by lauding the extent of a prince's greatness, power and riches, and the less a prince understands his responsibilities, the more eagerly he will embrace their message. Blinded as they are, such princes don't see that people who applaud them and pretend to approve of their behaviour usually intend to betray them later, holding them up to ridicule and exposing them to the hatred of their people. Aiding the cruelty, covetousness and lust of a prince is the surest way to betray him because he can't condemn the traitor without condemning himself.

> When the Franks, with the help of Aetius (then governing Gaul for the Romans), expelled King Clodion the Hairy from his kingdom, one of Clodion's friends who wanted him back on the throne succeeded in becoming close to Aetius. The story goes that he encouraged the avarice and cruelty to which this Roman was already disposed, and when he finally became insufferable, the Franks at once invited their king back to his kingdom. This counsellor realized that there was no surer way to betray his king's enemy than by encouraging him to pursue his vices.

> Sejanus, in his efforts to take over the Roman Empire, used this technique when he saw that Tiberius (who at his urging had imprisoned Agrippina and her children) had grown weary of the city and wanted to retire to Capri. Sejanus reinforced this desire because, while his master was away, the government of the state would be his. This is, in fact, what happened: for a while, Tiberius appeared to be the prince of only a little island while Sejanus acted as emperor of Rome itself.

> Perrennius did away with everyone who could oppose him under the guise of pursuing the accomplices of Lucilla, who had led a conspiracy against the emperor Commodus. He then plunged this emperor into all the delights and pleasures that he could, leaving himself free to take over the executive reins of government and ultimately to usurp the empire.

Bardas, the uncle of Michael III, emperor of Constantinople, made use of the same tactic. He ordered the assassination of Theoktistos, a fellow tutor, and then convinced the prince to banish his mother, Theodora, and take over the government himself. Then, being a man without honour, Bardas diverted Michael in the basest of ways, bathing him in vain delights and sexual pleasures and making him believe that there was no pastime more worthy than that of driving a coach or any accomplishment greater than that of being a skilful coachman. Meanwhile, Bardas gained the love of the people, recruiting many wise men and restoring Constantinople's schools and scholarship in all kinds of sciences. He was in line to take over the imperial throne and would have done so had he not been prevented by another.

A Warning to Princes

This is not encouragement to you to betray your prince but rather a warning to princes: be on your guard and don't think that a counsellor who encourages your debauchery or praises your ill-intentioned or inept initiatives cares for you any more than one who's prepared to rebuke you for such behaviour.

DEALING WITH
THOSE AROUND
YOUR PRINCE

DEALING WITH THE PRINCE'S PERSONAL SERVANTS

A Privileged Position

A prince's personal servants, by the nature of their responsibilities, are normally close to his person when he's in his private chambers. For this reason, they may be useful to you, by

- helping you gain access to the prince outside normal hours,
- putting in a good word for you when he mentions you,
- advising you on when and how to conduct your business, or
- advising you of favours you might be able to obtain.

Most princes wear a very a different face in public than they do in private. Once they've come to trust their personal servants, they open up more willingly in front of them, believing that they wouldn't dare try to exploit their princely confidences given their humble condition and their debt to their master.

> Everybody knows how Claudius was controlled by his freedmen. He had so enriched Pallas, one of these former slaves, that when he later lamented his own poverty, he was told that if he wanted to become wealthy, he should have Pallas adopt him. Agrippina appealed to this same Pallas when she wanted to snare the emperor into marrying her. Narcissus, another freedman of this prince, was the one who persuaded him to have Messalina put to death.

> We also know the power that the eunuchs held over the emperors of Greece, under whom they effectively ruled the empire. Without the assistance of Constantine's eunuchs and valets, Chancellor Arbetio might have lost his life when indicted by Count Verissimus.

Emperor Botoniates of Constantinople allowed two ordinary *valets de chambre*, Borilus and Germanus, to govern, and they worked against Isaac and Alexios Comnenus.

It's hard for a prince to keep his true face masked when alone with his servants. His true intentions escape much more clearly in private; when he's on public display in front of the people, he hides them with more care and restraint.

No One Too Humble

It's common for courtiers to recruit the assistance of individuals of all kinds and to be convinced that a person's prudence and discretion will grow in proportion to their increasing authority and fortune.

> Arrian illustrates this in his transcription of Epictetus with the example of one Epaphroditus and two of his slaves, one of whom had become valet of the bedchamber responsible for the emperor's urinal and commode, and the other a shoemaker. Epaphroditus had sold these two servants at one point, not knowing what to do with them, but then bought them back and cultivated their favour, praising their counsel and prudence.

Whatever else may be true about the court, you must understand that while you won't find any great friends there, neither will you find an enemy you can consider insignificant: anyone can help or hinder you, whatever his position.

> While Sejanus was in favour in the court of Tiberius, it was considered a great benefit to be known to Sejanus' doormen.

So if you're wise, you'll befriend the prince's personal servants and help them in any way that the rules of good conduct permit.

DEALING WITH GREAT NOBLES

There are several sorts of great nobles at court.

Some have nothing more to sustain them than their family name and a certain hereditary nobility or greatness; they are not close to the prince and have no executive authority. Others are less well positioned but have more executive power, and still others are both close to the prince and enjoy executive authority.

NOT CLOSE TO THE PRINCE, NO AUTHORITY

Those in this first category may be of little help to your getting ahead, but you should nevertheless cultivate relationships with them and treat them with respect. This you should do in part out of duty and in part to prevent them from damaging you. Though they can't hurt you much personally, they can still do so through their friends and servants. Great families always have people who depend on them or who are eager to please them, either

- because of some obligation for benefits previously bestowed,
- out of fear of their greatness, or
- in the hope that these great men will, given the vagaries of fortune, return to favour, making their patronage that much more valuable.

> Archelaus, king of Cappadocia, neglected to pay his respects to Tiberius when he was living quietly in Rhodes, much to his later disadvantage. When Tiberius subsequently came to power, he remembered this slight and took his revenge, accusing Archelaus of a trumped-up charge that caused the old man to die of regret. Yet it was not out of disdain that Archelaus had not visited Tiberius but because he had

feared the jealousy of Augustus had he showed himself to be a friend of Tiberius while Caius Caesar was still alive.

You must also understand that the means of such great nobles are never so diminished that they can't harm you, even if they don't have the means to help you. Even if your prince mistrusts them, you should still find some plausible excuse to get close to them. If you don't, you'll have to accept that they will be your enemies.

Opposing These Nobles

When you see that, as often happens, your prince's intention in promoting you is to set you against great men like these, you'll have to proceed with great art, skill and careful timing. You will need both to satisfy your prince and justify your actions to others. If you're promoted by your prince for this purpose, you can do one of two things:

- carry out the task you've been given so boldly that anyone you come up against (other than a great noble) will rally behind you for fear of offending the prince, or
- wait on the prince more closely; stick close to him and make the most of any opportunities that may arise for you to serve him, protect the poor or serve the public interest: you will be universally praised, and your reputation will grow.

Follow Through

You must be careful not to start something you can't finish. Common people judge actions by their results and always blame a loser. No matter who is truly to blame, if you fail at a task, you'll put your prince's reputation, and consequently his favour towards you, at risk. If he wants to avoid the disgrace of failing to complete what he started, he'll have to let you go. Even if your prince is prepared to accept his share of responsibility, this will inevitably lead to his being blamed by his subjects, which will fuel the determination of whoever he put you up against.

Avoid Confrontation

When I talk about your going up against great persons, I don't mean to imply that you should challenge them to a duel, for this can't be done without disrupting the affairs of state. Even less should you insult or speak ill of them, since such behaviour is only for people of poor judgment whose good fortune has left them so drunk that they are robbed of all common sense and understanding. Such men usually end up badly.

> This was what happened to Gnaeus Piso, who Tiberius sent into Syria to blunt the ambitions of Germanicus and balance out his power: he behaved so insolently that after the death of Germanicus, Tiberius was obliged to abandon him to the hatred of the people.

When to Oppose

I do, however, encourage you to oppose the projects of such great men when they can be considered

- evil in intent,
- against the interests of the government,
- a danger to public order,
- not in the best interests of justice,
- a risk to national security, or
- as endangering the treasury of the nation.

Even under these circumstances, you should try to justify your actions to all concerned and to all good men who may ask you about them. You should demonstrate that what you do is driven by a desire to do the right thing and not by personal ambition.

> If I had to suggest a recent example for you to model yourself on, it would be that of Cardinal Jimenez. Isabella, queen of Castile, hand-picked him to go up against a group of great Spanish nobles, who were not as obedient to their sovereign as they are now. Jimenez began his career as a Franciscan friar and was appointed confessor to the queen. Later, at the urging of Cardinal Mendoza, he was appointed Mendoza's successor as archbishop of Toledo and shortly thereafter was named head of the Spanish Inquisition to give him greater authority. He was so successful that he retained these offices not only under Isabella but later under Ferdinand of Aragon. After Ferdinand's death, he was sole arbiter and moderator of all the affairs of Spain until the arrival of the new emperor, Charles. He was constantly wrestling with the great nobles but always managed to keep his prince and the people on his side during all the quarrels and differences of opinion. It's reported that he was poisoned (he himself suspected it), but this was never proved and seems unlikely, as he was very old when he died. Regardless, this possibility doesn't diminish his good fortune, which he owed at least in part to his exemplary behaviour.
>
> Chico Simoneta, who managed the affairs of Milan for Francis Sforza and later his son Galeace, was not so successful. Because of his trustworthiness, he was selected to neutralize Galeace's brothers and govern the state during the regency of the queen mother while her son was a minor. To protect the throne for his pupil, Simoneta was obliged to banish Galeace's brothers and Robert de Saint Severin from Milan. After a short time, though, the queen mother reconciled with her other two sons, which proved to be at the expense of poor Simoneta, whom she abandoned to his enemies. They first imprisoned him and later had him put to a cruel death at the castle of Pavia.

Fickle Princes

Let this be a lesson to us all about how dangerous it is to perform the service of opposing great nobles for a fickle and superficial prince. For the smallest of reasons, such men are prone to dismiss those who have served them well and abandon them to the mercy of their enemies.

CLOSE TO THE PRINCE, NO AUTHORITY

Nobles who are in favour with and close to the prince but don't enjoy any executive authority can at least facilitate your access to him, even if they can't help you in other ways. They can also advance your cause by reminding him of your past services, excusing your inadvertent errors and defending you from slander and criticism. So although they can't promote you personally, if they're really your friends, they can point you in the direction of good and useful offices that can help you move up. If, however, they are against you, they can do you great harm and cause you to fall far from the good graces of your prince.

Win Them Over

You must use every means compatible with your status to become valued by men such as these. You should also understand that it's very difficult for men in their position to retain princely favour based only on familiarity. But even if a prince has decided not to give such counsellors any executive responsibility, he'll seldom refuse their recommendation to promote a person he can relate to and sees could serve him well. While they can't make the appointment themselves, influential men like these can see to it that their nominee gets appointed instead of another with equal or better qualifications.

Not Close to the Prince, Great Authority

Nobles in this third category are in offices of high authority with great executive power, yet have little access to their princes.

These men tend to be found around the kinds of princes who live a peaceful existence or who are wholly addicted to their own pleasures. Such princes are incapable of managing their own affairs, so they neglect them and delegate their responsibilities to one or more people they trust. They mostly avoid meeting with these counsellors for fear of having to listen to them talk business, which they consider a burden even to think about.

Influence Them Directly

In a context like this, you need to influence the servants rather than the master. The prince leaves the management of his affairs in their hands and most often leaves the selection of subordinate officers to them also; since he understands nothing of business, he's incapable of judging what it takes for someone to succeed at it.

Reach the Prince

There are other princes in this category who are more protective of their state and majesty. Though they may entrust their affairs to one or two executives, they don't allow them to become too close or familiar and seldom, if ever, meet or talk with them except to check up on what they're doing and to make the important decisions. Such princes do not let their ministers fill more junior positions with their own people, fearing that through these dependants they may amass so much power and so many servants that if they do step out of line, they'll be too powerful to depose.

This kind of prince desires above all to have his ministers live in fear of him and likes them to feel that, in the blink of an eye, he's willing to ruin someone he promoted slowly over the years. It's hard to know how to behave towards great nobles who find themselves in this situation. Their goodwill can be of little use to you; on the contrary, it can harm you if the prince becomes aware of it. But if you don't cultivate relationships with them, you may find yourself blocked from promotion to positions of responsibility and will have to face the many difficulties and obstacles they can throw in your way.

Courtiers like this require a gentle touch. You must treat them with the utmost respect and, whenever possible, demonstrate your loyalty by providing them with assistance in secret and services unseen by others.

Look Elsewhere

Meanwhile, though, you must seek out the support of someone more valued by your prince—someone able to introduce you to him and help you gain access.

CLOSE TO THE PRINCE, GREAT AUTHORITY

There remains a last category of noblemen who are, in short, the favourites: they are both highly favoured by the prince and occupy important positions.

Court Them

You should court men like this rather than courting the prince himself. To succeed, you need to understand their agendas and to get behind them rather than whatever the prince himself may want. You must also carefully determine now much princely favour each of your potential patrons among these great nobles enjoys.

Ask Only for What's Possible

No matter their goodwill towards you, never ask one of these nobles for something you think may be (or even may seem to them to be) impossible for them to deliver. Nothing is more vexing than having to refuse a petition from a friend, and it's an affront to their goodwill to set it in conflict with an impossible or unreasonable request.

Remember that a great man who's had to refuse you such a request won't be pleased to see you again. He'll fear that you'll embarrass him a second time with a similar demand and make him look as though he lacks the means and authority to help you.

Be Patient

If you don't have easy access to these great nobles, you must work to obtain it one step at a time. To do this, you must win over their family members or anyone else who has any influence over them. Seek out the people who depend on them and, given the degree of their dependence and the influence they have, evaluate the power that each has to help you.

DEALING WITH LESSER COURTIERS

In any court, there are those of lesser rank than the great nobles. Some of these will be your betters, some your equals and some your inferiors, and you should pay all of them close attention.

Those Who May Help You

Just as with great nobles, you must weigh the status and influence of each lesser courtier given what you want to achieve. You must also consider the power and favour of the people who depend on them for reasons of family connections, goodwill or obligation.

Certain matters are better broached with your friends by one of their own circle rather than by you, either to guarantee that your request will be well received or to get around anyone who may be trying to stop you.

It's important that you don't wait to start cultivating these friendships until you obviously have need of them. You should win such friends well in advance and secure their support by doing things for them and providing other proof of your goodwill.

Those Who May Hurt You

Those that may hurt you are typically of three kinds

- your enemies,
- those that envy[35] you, or
- those that are in healthy competition with you.

Your Friends' Enemies

Your adversaries may either hate you personally or hate you because you're a friend of an enemy of theirs. If they hate your friends, their enmity for you will usually be less sharp, and you can greatly mitigate this kind of hatred by doing something to show that your love for your friends doesn't prevent you from being their friend as well. This said, partiality is usually so rife in the courts of princes, and the humours and friendships of great men so tyrannical, that it can be hard to remain openly neutral for long.

For this reason, many have publicly supported one side in a dispute while secretly maintaining relations with people on the other. They don't do this to betray whoever they're publicly supporting but as a form of personal insurance should their friends fall. While betrayal would be below a man of honour, a secret friendship like this has no goal other than legitimate self-preservation and so should not be rejected.

The exercise of this kind of prudence has been reported in the machinations of both courts and kingdoms.

> Syenneses, governor of Tarsus for the king of Persia, saw that Artaxerxes was being attacked by Cyrus but couldn't oppose him without risking certain defeat. So instead, he publicly backed him and, as protection should he lose, sent his son to join Artaxerxes.

> When Bardas Durus escaped from the Saracens, he discovered that his enemy Bordas Phocus had been made emperor instead of Basilius. Wanting to secure his relationships with both sides, he courted Phocus' friendship but sent his son to Basilius, pretending that he had been stolen away without his knowledge. In this way, if Phocus fell from power, Bardas Durus could still be reconciled with the new emperor, which is in fact what happened.

> Solon introduced a law that provided that no person could remain neutral on matters of state business. He did not intend that friends

who found themselves on opposite sides of a debate should sacrifice their personal friendships; on the contrary, the basic principle of this legislation was to ensure that friends with conflicting viewpoints would find constructive and amicable ways to resolve their differences.

You should keep your friends, whatever their opinions may be. This will ensure not only that you have support in times of difficulty, but also that you will be well placed to mediate between the two factions when time and circumstances permit.

This is the safest and most commendable position to take when living through the quarrels and animosities of great men, as well as the best way to sustain your friendships with everyone involved.

Your Enemies

If someone hates you personally, it is either

- because he has offended you, which is often why great men hate their inferiors; in the words of the Italian proverb, "he that offends never forgives," or
- because you have offended him.

He Offended You

So far as the first category is concerned, if someone has injured you, it's best to appear not to have taken offence. If the insult is so great that it can't go unnoticed, you must show that time has softened memory and that you have forgotten about it. If you appear to be still angry, the person who hurt you will believe that you want revenge, and this will provoke him to try to hurt you every chance he gets.

In particular, you must avoid making threats. You'd be an idiot to issue a threat unless and until you're ready to exact vengeance. Otherwise, your threat will both put your adversary on his guard and, as I have said, invite him to attack you again. Besides, threatening revenge without having the power to exact it will only display your weakness and bring you nothing but shame.

I realize that this kind of moderation isn't to everyone's liking, especially to those unforgiving characters who think no injury should go unchallenged. These people revel in the sweetness of revenge and believe that you should never forgive someone who has hurt you because suffering one offence in silence only invites another. In their efforts to be formidable adversaries, however, these individuals only succeed in making everyone flee their company. We mortals are prone to slips and falls and are carried away at times by carelessness and at others by passion; so we seek to avoid such vindictive people for fear of offending them and being added to their list of enemies. Even a person who does associate with someone like this, when he realizes that he has somehow given offence, will drop the unforgiving character for good, leaving him alone to his solitude like a wild beast.

Knowing that people like this will try to hurt you, you must do everything in your power to anticipate their actions and prevent them.

Seek Reconciliation

To avoid the ill will of such people, I suggest that you take the opposite approach and seek reconciliation, even for the greatest of wrongs.

If you have been offended, you should analyze the motivation and sometimes the social standing of the one who has wronged you.

- In the case of minor wrongs, especially those that spring more from sudden passion than from malice, you should appear so indifferent to them that it's impossible for anyone to tell that you've noticed them at all.

- If the injury is really outrageous, you mustn't appear unmindful of your honour and reputation. On the other hand, you shouldn't react so fiercely that whoever wronged you believes he has no chance of ever being forgiven or reconciled with you. While you show your displeasure, you should also hint at the possibility of making up and leave a door open to some appropriately easy satisfaction. You should even take your complaint to his friends and let them be the judge of what he has done to you.

- If the offence is given in an aggressive and domineering way, you should deal with it on the spot if possible. This is not so much to get revenge as to punish the offender and teach him to treat you and others better in the future. As before, you shouldn't appear to have excluded any possibility of eventual forgiveness. On the contrary, you should make it clear that it was only with the greatest regret that you found yourself forced to react and seek redress and that you're prepared to make up as soon as you've been appropriately compensated. If you don't receive a timely public or private apology but the offender seems to be truly sorry or humbly asks you for a favour, you should make up with him. Be satisfied with the request of the person who criticized and offended you, for it acknowledges his need of you.

People More Powerful

Because you are usually wronged by people more powerful than you:

- The first way to avoid conflict is to treat these powerful men with respect, taking no liberties and not annoying them by staying continually at their side. If they become very rough and angry, try to avoid them altogether.

- The second tactic is to patiently give the impression that you've noticed nothing wrong. It's neither safe nor prudent to respond with defiance or threats that are out of proportion to the power of those who have offended you: the inequality of power alone is sufficient excuse for you to feign ignorance.

Intimidation

I know that some people are convinced that if you scare or intimidate those who've offended you, you can push them into considering making up with you. I won't deny that this can sometimes work with the less principled sort of person, but a reconciliation you come to by this means can never be trusted. People without principles will always try to get back at you if they can, and it's a lot harder to anticipate a secret enemy than a public one; it's better to have overt enemies than false friends who've been pressured into reconciliation.

I should point out that this rule applies only when you're dealing with people no more powerful than you, and whose friendship you can do without. With someone who's capable of obstructing your business and putting you down, a sham reconciliation is better than open hostility.

You Injured Him

If you have wronged another person, because you're at fault, it's up to you to find a way, in person or through your friends, to make things right.

Revenge and Fear

To determine how much harm someone can do to you, you have to consider both how powerful he is and what is motivating him (other than plain dislike) to obstruct you.

- Some are driven by hate to seek vengeance.
- Others fear that their plans will be compromised if you reach your goals.

Though the desire for vengeance is always very violent, fear will drive an adversary to oppose you with even greater passion. For this reason, it is far harder to divert someone who is driven by fear than someone who is driven by hatred.

You may be able to overcome someone's desire for revenge by offering him commissions, services and reparations. But you will have great difficulty making a fearful and insecure person come to feel secure. The only way to achieve this is to make peace with him and rebuild his trust in you through friendship. You will have to make the most of whatever opportunities present themselves, though, because you won't be able to plan in advance.

> To reconcile with his enemies and make a show of helping, Agesilaus appointed people he had quarrelled with to important offices and had them given executive positions of great authority. But because in their new positions they found it hard to satisfy everyone, their performance was criticized, they were accused of incompetence and

they finally had to seek Agesilaus' protection. He sheltered them from punishment and blame, thereby earning their sincere friendship.

It's a common trick at court to stick your leg out to trip someone so that later you can help them to their feet and thereby earn their gratitude and bind them to you.

Encouraging Excess

There is an even more common trick, much used on enemies, that you should look out for. This is illustrated by the skill and finesse of Eutrapel as recounted by Horace. Eutrapel lent money on credit, advanced money for fine clothes and inflated the egos of those he wanted to ruin.

In summary, anyone who

- encourages your amorous adventures,
- applauds your fits of anger,
- encourages your spending habits, or
- praises you more than you deserve, puffing you up to attempt things beyond all sense and reason

usually does these things to harm rather than help you.

Side With Them

To come back to how you can renew your friendships with your enemies, whenever you see that you're not going to be able to stop them from doing something, join with them and help them.

This is what Cardinal Ascanius Sforza did when he saw the futility of opposing Cardinal Julian's schemes to promote Pope Alexander VI's young son John. He promoted the boy so enthusiastically that John owed his cardinal's cap more to him than to Julian and became his friend.

It is wise to support what you can't prevent and to cut your suit according to your cloth.

If you can't find any way to make peace with an enemy or if your attempts to reassure him or to soften his attitude towards you fail, consider how he really feels about you and identify someone he hates and fears more than you. Then, have this other person's name mentioned as a competitor to both you and your enemy. This way, the hatred your enemy has for this third person may induce him to favour you more, or at least to oppose you less.

> Gerlachus, archbishop and elector of Mainz, used this strategy to get his cousin Adolphus of Nassau elected emperor at a time when none of the electors would have voted for him. He knew that all the candidates were at odds with each other, so he dealt separately and secretly with each elector. He told Wenceslaus, the king of Bohemia, that the electors' votes would favour his enemy Albert, duke of Austria, but that if he'd give him power of attorney to vote for someone else, he'd do all he could to prevent Albert's election. Gerlachus then dealt the same way with the elector of Saxony, suggesting that his enemy the duke of Brunswick would likely win. Then he assured the count palatine that his enemy Wenceslaus, king of Bohemia, would likely be elected. By this means, he extracted a power of attorney from each elector, promised to block the election of each of their enemies, and elected his cousin, who had not even been in the running.

DEALING WITH PEOPLE WHO ENVY YOU

Dealing with people who envy you takes a great deal of determination and courage. The destructive vice of envy, it is said, can be softened by giving away or sharing the object that is envied. No matter how much you may want to keep what you get for yourself, sometimes this is not possible.

Mutual Advantage

What I think can be done, though, is to avoid sharing what you're after by convincing your competitor that it would work to his advantage (it'd support his aims, it'd be convenient for him) for you to win the prize. Even if his jealousy and ill-will are obvious, you must court him with friendship and familiarity and find ways to express your strong affection for him. Convince him that he wants you to succeed because this will put you in a better position to help him. Show that you only want to succeed so you can help your friends, not least himself.

Don't Show Off

Another remedy for envy is to avoid showing off, and to avoid

- excessive spending,
- frivolity,
- flashy, unnecessary celebrations, and
- too many parties.

Those who've risen from humble beginnings need to tread most carefully here. The only exception to this rule is if your prince, or the dignity of your office, obliges you to make some outward show. Even in these circumstances, though, it's prudent to show the world that you'd be reluctant to go to all this expense if it weren't for your obligation to your prince.

> Cardinal Jimenez's early career was marked by this kind of modesty and prudence. He was said to have been born of lowly parents, though others have written that he was born a gentleman. Whatever the truth, Jimenez began his career as a friar and, when his talents were recognized by Cardinal Archbishop Mendoza of Toledo, was promoted on the latter's recommendation to be confessor to

Queen Isabella of Castile. Not long afterwards, also on the recommendation of the cardinal, he was named archbishop of Toledo as a counterweight to the power of the realm's great nobles. Following Mendoza's death, the queen sought the necessary papal bulls from Rome to confirm his appointment as archbishop. Jimenez refused these, judging that were he to occupy this high office, he would attract more envy from the great nobles of the realm than he would be able to resist. To convince him to accept the appointment, the queen eventually had to send all the nobles from her court. When after several refusals he finally agreed, Jimenez was still reluctant to increase the size of his household or his estate to a level befitting his new position, whatever anyone said to him. In the end, only the pope's express command could induce him to change. This modesty served him well, and he avoided the envy that otherwise would have come with this powerful position, coveted by all the great nobles of Spain, and enjoyed revenues as great as, or greater than, those of most princes.

But while this approach can be an antidote to envy in the early days of a career, it is of little use to someone who has already shown himself to be more ambitious than humble.

It was of no use, for example, to Constantin Mesopolitain when, after his banishment from the courts of the emperors Isaac and then Alexios Angelos of Constantinople, he returned with Empress Euphrosyne pretending that he no longer wanted any hand in state business. To prove his point, he went so far as to join the church as a deacon to give himself an excuse to turn down promotions at court, which only made people want him more. In short, he played this role so well that the emperor himself obtained a dispensation from John Xiphilinus, patriarch of Constantinople, allowing him to accept an executive position at court as he had before, despite the church canons and decrees that forbade this. Mesopolitain soon brought in two of his brothers, who from then on stayed stuck to the emperor's side when business called Mesopolitain away. But his ploy was short-lived: everyone already knew that Mesopolitain was a devious and ambitious character, and he was banished again, later to die far from court.

DEALING WITH COMPETITORS

The same route you need to take to defend yourself from envy will help you deal with the healthier competition of emulation. Emulation is less malignant than envy but betrays a sharper ambition and will cause you no less trouble.

Boost Their Self-image

Those who feel compelled to compete with you will not be won over by shows of respect or veneration. You can, however, coax them onto a different path by

- encouraging them to aim for a goal more ambitious than yours,
- helping them achieve this goal,
- offering to help advance their ambitions, and
- playing down your own goal as being too insignificant for them to aspire to.

Imply that you have no choice but to pursue your goal because you aren't capable of competing (as they are) for anything better. By way of contrast, praise your competitors' reputation, power, abilities and merit: suggest that they can do far better than you and should set their sights higher.

Sow Doubts

If ever you come to fear that a competitor may get ahead of you, raise doubts and insecurities in his mind about what he wants to do. Discuss the pros and cons of the matter, but always in a way that reinforces why he should give up and look elsewhere.

BE DISCREET

Your best and quickest course, though, is to disguise or hide your objective until it's too late for anyone to compete with you or block you.

Pushing an ambitious plan too openly may repel the very people who would have helped you if you'd been more discreet, making your task more difficult and damaging your chances of success. Then, if you do prevail, you'll attract more envy than you would have otherwise, and if you fail, you'll look that much more foolish. Your safest course is to do as rowers do, turning your back on your objective and showing every sign of having some other destination.

This method has often been used by those with aspirations to command, imitating Euripides' Agamemnon by expressing a greater interest in retirement than in the burdens of high office. This technique

- can protect you against the obstacles that might be thrown in your path if your true intentions were known,
- will enable you to avoid the shame normally attached to someone who fails to reach his objective, and
- should you succeed, will cause your success to be attributed more to your merit than to your scheming.

AVOID STRONGER RIVALS

But beware. If you want to succeed, don't use this approach with anyone who's more powerful or enjoys more support than you, even if you think you can win.

> Imitate M. Lepidus, who Tacitus regarded as a very wise courtier. When Tiberius brought this Lepidus into the Senate to run against

Sejanus' uncle Junius Blaesus for proconsul of Africa, Lepidus declined the honour, citing his poor health and the young age of his children, including even that one of his daughters was about to be married. In reality, though, he feared that in such a competition, he would have had to attack the reputation and power of Blaesus and that if he won (which was entirely possible), he would make an enemy of Sejanus.

In particular, never get carried away and oppose a qualified candidate who is sponsored by a prince, even if law and natural justice are on your side. In such cases, a prince's patronage always comes before the law.

This is what happened when Germanicus and Drusus campaigned for Haterius Agrippa to become praetor and succeeded in having him appointed by the Senate, despite this being illegal.

AVOIDING A FALL
FROM FAVOUR

BE PREPARED

Up to this point, we've reviewed the principal precepts you should follow to succeed at court: the rest must come from your own judgment and dexterity. And while following these rules will certainly help you hold on to your position, you can also learn from studying the cases of courtiers who have fallen from favour in the past. Analyzing what damaged the careers of others will allow you to avoid, anticipate or prevent the same things from happening to you; and if worst comes to worst, you will at least be able to prepare yourself for them.

Since efforts to escape impending misfortune are, for the most part, in vain, it's no less necessary for you to prepare for a fall from favour than it is to struggle to maintain your position. A fall from favour is normal and virtually inevitable for anyone who fortune has lifted so high, and being prepared can make your fall far easier and gentler than it would otherwise have been.

A fall from grace or a reduction in the regard your prince has for you can come about through

- your own failings,
- the malice, spite or competition of enemies,
- the perverseness of your prince's nature, or
- your prince's death.

THROUGH YOUR OWN FAILINGS

The behaviour of all men is plagued by imperfections and failings. This is particularly true of those who believe themselves to be above others and who've reached that point where not only does no one dare contradict them, but where they can use their authority to get their entourage to applaud their faults and errors.

TREASON

Plots against a prince's person or realm by someone he promoted to a position of power are those most deserving of his condemnation. Such treason demonstrates an extreme ingratitude and infidelity and consequently provides a prince with the best reason of all to ruin the perpetrator. Anyone fortunate enough to be thus raised up should therefore avoid giving his prince any cause to mistrust him, and to this end should distance himself from the pursuit of any honours or positions that might cast a shadow of suspicion on him.

> Velleius Paterculus considered Sejanus to have been one of the wisest and most capable courtiers ever to attend the court of Tiberius, which indeed he must have been to hold the favour of such a clever and mistrustful prince. He was always busy, we're told, but behaved as though he was doing little, giving the impression that everything came easily to him. He never boasted but got everything done, was self-deprecating, and acted more modestly than the high opinion others had of him would have justified. His outwardly cool and poised behaviour disguised a vigilant and watchful spirit. Eventually, though, ambition drove him to seek the hand of Drusus' widow Livia in marriage in the hopes that joining the household of the Caesars might constitute the first step on a ladder to help him realize his ambitions to control

the empire. When his request for Tiberius' consent met with vigorous opposition and considerable suspicion (largely because of the early wedding date he'd requested), he didn't give up on his ultimate objective but adopted an alternative approach.

Seeing that Tiberius had grown weary of the city, Sejanus helped persuade him to retire to Capri. This, he hoped, would reduce his master's jealousy of the way the great nobles courted him in Rome and the extent to which they envied him. It would also increase his power, since all state business would then have to pass through his hands. Letters were sent through the soldiers of the guard under his command, and he could give or deny access to anyone he wanted. He was soon able, on the pretext of easing the burdens on the aging Tiberius, to take over all the affairs of state and to consolidate what appeared to be a firm and powerful position. But Sejanus was dealing with a prudent prince, and subsequent events show that the path he'd chosen was more hazardous than beneficial for him.

I think it's relevant to look at what followed, both to warn courtiers to be more prudent in how they advance their careers, and to warn princes to be more careful how they dispense their favours.

Tiberius tolerated Sejanus' behaviour for as long as his tactics and tricks were needed to keep Agrippina and her sons Nero and Drusus under control. Sejanus had set about this task with extra enthusiasm, knowing that it would set Tiberius' mind at rest and that it would help him advance in the emperor's good graces. He would be increasing his own power at the same time, making himself that much more formidable and making his eventual seizure of power that much more likely. The house of Caesar at that time had no alternative candidate, only children too young to get in his way and control of whom represented a potential springboard to enable him to take over the state. He could effectively control them and set himself up to rule in their names until his own position became unassailable.

But more often than not, ambition is indiscreet and rash, and Sejanus didn't see that the closer he came to reaching his objective, the more suspicion he was kindling in his mistrustful prince. To stay in Tiberius' good graces, he should have looked to reduce rather than increase his power, but he failed to realize this. All he had left to aspire to was the title of emperor (which many of his followers already accorded him) and the power of tribune, which previous emperors had consolidated with their own authority, allowing them to rule absolutely. Sejanus tried to appropriate more and more power for himself, becoming feared by all and suspect to his prince. Tiberius saw that Sejanus had used gifts, hope and fear to win over the imperial Praetorian Guard and a great number of the senators and best families of Rome. Indeed, even his own personal servants were reporting everything he said and did to Sejanus, while none of them dared tell him what Sejanus was up to. Before taking any action, though, Tiberius felt it prudent to canvass the opinions of those around him and establish who he could and could not trust to support him.

To reach his goal more smoothly and to prevent Sejanus from becoming suspicious, Tiberius made him consul and called him his "friend and companion" in his letters to both the Senate and the people. After a time, he feigned a terminal illness in part to see who reacted to the news with joy and who with sorrow, but principally to watch the reactions and gauge the ambitions of Sejanus and his confederates. Sometimes he would write that he was recovering and would soon return to Rome. In his letters he also alternately praised and belittled Sejanus, promoting some of his followers but demoting or hindering others, thereby keeping Sejanus suspended between hope and fear. So Sejanus took no action, not wanting to gamble the honour and favour that he thought were his on some decisive move and trusting the passage of time to enable him to erase these trivial dissatisfactions. In the interim, though, his less faithful followers and those who were only attracted to his success realized that Tiberius' favour for him was wavering and began to distance themselves from him bit by bit as his star waned.

Tiberius became concerned that all of this might incite the ambitious Sejanus to make his move sooner, so he lulled him into a false sense of security by putting it about that he intended to make him tribune. Only a short while later, Tiberius wrote letters to the Senate ordering the arrest of Sejanus and assigned Macro, the captain of the guard, to deliver them. When Macro arrived in Rome, he went immediately to deliver the emperor's orders first to the consul Mummius Regalus (the other consul being a creature of Sejanus) and then, still before dawn, to Graecinus Laco, the captain of the watch. Later in the morning, he went to present Tiberius' letters at the palace where he met Sejanus, who, greatly worried, asked if there weren't any letters for him from the emperor. Macro, to reassure him, whispered in his ear as though it were a great secret that he was carrying a decree appointing him tribune. Sejanus, pleased and happy, entered the Senate escorted by the Praetorian Guard, who Macro then dismissed, passing on

Tiberius' order that they should return to camp and showing them his letters that promised them a cash bonus for their obedience. In their place, he stationed the soldiers of the watch and then entered the Senate and delivered his letters. He left before they were opened, having ordered Laco to make sure Sejanus didn't try to escape or stir up any sedition. He then went to the camp of the Praetorian Guard to make sure they understood where their duty lay.

The letters that Tiberius had sent to the Senate were skilfully crafted and purposely very long-winded to give Macro time to carry out all his orders. They began with no mention of Sejanus, referring instead to various other matters. This was followed by a brief and mild complaint about Sejanus, which was followed again by other matters, and then again by a very brief criticism of Sejanus. Then, in the midst of various other topics, Tiberius ordered that two senators, friends of Sejanus, be punished and that Sejanus himself be arrested. At this point, because there had purposely been no mention of a death sentence and because all the accusations against him had been minor and unimportant, Sejanus retained the hope that he could come through largely unscathed.

Once the reading of the letters had concluded, many of those who had accompanied Sejanus to the Senate saw that he had not been named tribune and began to close in around him to keep him from escaping, which he would likely have attempted had the emperor's letters been any harsher in their accusations. As it was, he saw little to fear from these trivial charges and stayed seated, only rising once Mummius Regulus had called on him to do so two or three times, not (according to Dio) out of pride but because he'd become unaccustomed to obeying orders. When he finally rose, Laco, captain of the watch, followed him. Regulus and the other magistrates also rose and escorted him out of the court and to prison. The Senate later sentenced him to be cast down from the place known as the Gemonian Stairs.

Thus fell one of the most skilful and powerful courtiers of all time; a fall that should be attributed more to the weight of the power he had amassed (which alone was enough to ruin him) than to the prudence and skill of his prince, great though this was.

Commodus, a man of far poorer judgment than Tiberius, demonstrated this with respect to Perennius, who followed the same path as Sejanus with (given the laziness of his prince) a far better chance of success.

I know that everyone who undertakes a treasonous venture of this kind thinks he's cleverer than the next man and has some special knack that will guarantee his success. Some have held to this belief right up to the point of putting their plan into action.

> An example was Boylas, who had carried out his plans reasonably competently but escaped the usual fate of such conspirators only because his emperor, Constantin Monomague of Constantinople, was a far milder prince than most and readily forgave those who wronged him.

This case shows that what's hidden from the eyes of man can be revealed by God in mysterious ways; however cleverly a subordinate moves against his leader, he who takes this path risks ruin.

> Boylas appeared to be a man above his prince's suspicion, not only because of the patronage he'd previously enjoyed but also because he had many handicaps that made him seem incapable of taking on anything ambitious. Not only was he of very mean birth, but he stammered so badly and spoke so unintelligibly that people could hardly understand him. Once he saw that the emperor liked to hear him talk like this, though, he exaggerated and regularly demonstrated his handicap, and by clowning like this eventually became so favoured that he had the run of his master's harem and his private chambers. His prince made him wealthy and made him a senator, but he still coveted more, to the point where he planned to murder his leader and seize the throne. To gather a following, he shared his plan first with those he was certain hated the emperor, making great promises to anyone who went along with him and would help him. He praised those whose loyalty and affection for the prince led them to reject his plan, claiming that he had propositioned them only to test their loyalty to the emperor (which he would confirm) and exhorting them to continue. In this way, he ensured that for a long time nobody realized what he was up to. Indeed, his plot would have succeeded had not one of the conspirators revealed it and ensured that he was placed under surveillance. Thanks to this, Boylas was caught in the act, sword in hand, ready to strike his master and kill him. Thus surprised, the emperor was content to banish him after having had some of his supporters punished.

It would take me forever to list all the great men whose careers have been shipwrecked at court, not only for actually perpetrating such treasons but also because others feared that they might do so. So I'll content myself for now with those I've mentioned.

JEALOUSY

A courtier tempts fate and risks ruin if he in any way displays that he is jealous of his prince, be it through

- ambition,
- boasting,
- criticism,
- denigration, or
- excessive displays of wealth.

> Boasting and telling of their services were the ruin of Philotas and Clytus at the court of Alexander.
>
> Craterus would have been held in much higher esteem had he acted less selfishly and more modestly.
>
> It is written that Silius lost his favour with Tiberius for this same reason.
>
> Josephus writes that Silva, general of King Agrippa's army, lost everything he'd gained from all his past services through trying to steal the credit for all victories from his leader.
>
> Antonius Primus ruined his reputation and his position with Vespasian through a similar show of vanity.

Princes see behaviour like this in their subordinates as an attack on their princely glory, which they consider to be attached to their person and not to be reflected in the worth, wealth or merit of a subject.

Criticism

Criticizing your prince or even complaining to him too insistently is indiscreet and often born of arrogance.

> Eumenes displeased King Alexander by complaining about how quarters usually reserved for the troops had been taken over by Hephaestion and his party of fools and jesters. Having spoken too freely, Eumenes then feared that he'd be disgraced.

Abuse of Familiarity

Abusing your leader's familiarity and presenting yourself as the one running his business can be interpreted as pride, though in fact some do this out of vanity and others out of greed.

> Zoticus' experience under the monstrous Elagabalus is an example of someone who had better luck than did Thurinus under Alexander, son of Julia Mamaea. Thurinus managed to get everyone at court to believe that he controlled his master and that all his actions could be attributed to his advice and counsel. He also bragged about the liberties he took with the prince, whether these were real or not. In the words of his executioner, the emperor had Thurinus "suffocated in smoke for selling smoke."

Greed

On the topic of greed directed at princes or great nobles, one of the most striking examples is the temerity, vanity and treachery of Plautianus.

> The presumption of Plautianus led him to oppose Bassianus, son of his master the emperor, the very man who had promoted him to the greatness he then enjoyed. He was so vain that when he travelled through the city, not only did no one dare approach him, but he sent people ahead to clear the streets where he would pass, forbidding anyone to dare set eyes on him. Ultimately, his arrogant blindness led him to plot treason against his prince and cost him his life.

> We also know how Enguerrand de Marigny, while in favour under Philip the Fair, plotted against Charles de Valois.

Division

Never let yourself become an instrument of division or conflict between two princes, for princes always reach agreement between themselves at the expense of whoever provoked their conflict.

> There are many examples of this, and the history of Bavaria provides that of a certain Otho Crondoserus, a favourite of Rudolph, palatine of the Rhine. He'd orchestrated a dispute between the prince and his mother, but when these two were eventually reconciled, they had his tongue torn off and his eyes put out.

Not Offending Favourites

In addition to avoiding conflict with princes, you should take care not to go up against or obstruct the career of anyone who enjoys more favour than you.

> On his deathbed, Germanicus advised Agrippina not to provoke the most powerful and favoured nobles. She ignored his advice, which proved to be the eventual cause of her ruin and that of her children.
>
> I have mentioned how Eumenes feared being disgraced by Alexander for having so rashly complained about Hephaestion. Besides his indiscretion, Eumenes also offended his leader by his irreverent remarks and the envy he thereby displayed of Hephaestion.

This is why it's so important for you to know how much of your prince's favour you enjoy compared to others, and not to judge this so much by external appearances as by the cause of the favour.

> For a while both Craterus and Hephaestion seemed to enjoy an equal measure of Alexander's favour, Alexander calling Craterus "the king's friend" and calling Hephaestion "Alexander's friend." Craterus should have understood that princes are generally more closely attached to their personal enjoyment and inclinations than they are to maintaining

the dignity of their position, and as a result, that someone who respects the dignity of their position, even if the prince likes him, is still less valued than a personal friend. Personal interests always touch a prince more closely than his dignity. When Craterus and Hephaestion got into an argument that divided the whole court, Alexander stayed neutral. He sharply criticized both men and threatened each with punishment if they ever quarrelled again. The way he dealt with them was evidence more of his prudence in extinguishing the problem (putting out the fire that would have raged if this split had continued) than that his regard for each of them was equal. He rebuked Hephaestion publicly to reduce the people's jealousy of him, and dealt with Craterus privately so that the majority of Macedonians, who were on his side, wouldn't be upset. This is how a prince should behave in circumstances such as this.

Coming back to the need I've outlined for you to evaluate the relative degree of favour you enjoy with your prince, you can see that one of the first mistakes Antonius Primus (mentioned above) made was to recklessly oppose Mucianus, who was more highly regarded by Vespasian than he, and who (Tacitus says) it was more dangerous to criticize than Vespasian himself.

Criticizing Favourites

In every court there is recognition that criticism of a prince's favourites is more strongly avenged than criticism of the prince himself: Dio demonstrates this when talking of Sejanus.

It's interesting to note that those who've earned their positions on merit don't seek out the hollow shows of honour and ceremony usually accorded to great nobles at court. Anyone who expects such outward signs of respect needs them to offset his own unworthiness to fill the position he's in, and will always take offence if not treated according to the protocol reserved for persons high in princely favour. As a result, a friendship with such a person is far harder to maintain than is the friendship and goodwill of a prince. A prince enhances his reputation by pardoning those who offend him, whereas someone who needs outward shows of respect thinks that offering forgiveness will make him look weak and scared. He believes the best way to demonstrate and consolidate his power is to punish and harass anyone who forgets his station or his duty.

Men of Lower Rank

Not only is arrogance towards great nobles very inappropriate, but arrogance has also ruined people who have taken on men of lower rank.

> John, King of Aragon, favoured Alvarez de Luna, Bastard of Aragon, so much that of his own accord, he stripped responsibility from the principal and greatest nobles of his realm and out of goodwill entrusted Alvarez with the management all his personal affairs and business. But Alvarez became so insolent that he had a gentleman thrown out of a window for approaching him with an unwanted message from the king, at which point John had him beheaded. Thus John punished this prince's pride.

Inciting Hatred

You will also fall from favour if you behave so arrogantly that you bring the hatred of the people or great nobles down on you or your leader. In these circumstances you must expect either that your prince will decide to get rid of you or that the courtiers around you will ruin you.

> Commodus was obliged to have his deputy Cleander executed to appease the feelings of the people of Rome, against whom he had armed the Praetorian Guard.
>
> Eutropius was the favourite of Arcadius, but when he caused the revolt of Tribigild, his prince was obliged to abandon him to his enemies to keep the peace.

> Anterus was envied and hated for the great favour in which he was
> held by Commodus, and the other servants of this emperor resolved
> to seize and kill this young man one evening when he returned to his
> lodgings; this they did.

BETRAYAL OF SECRETS

Another common reason for a courtier's downfall, and certainly
one of the most deserved, is the betrayal of a prince's secrets and
conspiracy with his enemies. This is one of the most common
failings and is often prompted as much by carelessness, indiscre-
tion and vanity as it is by infidelity.

Carelessness

With respect to carelessness, I believe the wisest thing a courtier
can do is to avoid learning any of a prince's secrets: never even
listen to them except in the company of others. If a prince divulges
some information to you alone and then somehow, in the normal
course of business, something close to what you were told starts
to circulate, the prince will immediately suspect you of having
leaked it. Even if he has shared the same information with someone else, whether he remembers doing it or not, he may consider
his other confidant to be more discreet. In that case, he will blame
you for the leak, even if the other person was responsible for it.

> Philippedes was a comic poet and the most highly favoured of the
> courtiers of King Lysimachus. When the king asked him what he
> most wanted to know, Philippedes replied, "Everything you wish to
> tell me . . . except your secrets."

You should never willingly burden yourself with something
that will be hard to keep safe.

In truth, you shouldn't even want to learn such secrets, whether directly from the prince or from someone with whom he may have shared them. Hiero, the prince of Syracuse, used to say that he who gives away a prince's secret harms both himself and he to whom he gave it, for a prince will hate without exception anyone who knows his secrets.

Conspiracy

Fortune has been no kinder to those, insiders or outsiders, who've conspired with a prince's enemies out of greed, ambition or in the hopes of making friends on both sides.

> Cardinal Balue, the son of a tailor, was appointed treasurer by Louis XI and from treasurer was made bishop. Eventually, he received a cardinal's hat from Pope Paul II, in part because the king requested it, but also in part because the pope wanted to win the gratitude of the man who'd been his adversary and prevent him from again undermining papal authority with the king. Later, however, it was discovered that the cardinal had conspired with the king's enemies. For this, Louis XI had him jailed in the Tower of Loches, and there he stayed for twelve years until released at the request of Pope Sixtus IV.

> During the reign of Francis I, Cardinal du Prat fell from favour for similar machinations and was also imprisoned. He was only released because he convinced all his doctors (by drinking his own urine) that he was suffering from urine retention, and the king was afraid of making an enemy of the pope should the cardinal die in prison.

> Pierre de Vignes, chief counsellor to Emperor Frederick II, did not get off so lightly. He was blinded on suspicion of plotting with his master's enemy, Pope Alexander III.

> Stilicho's death, it is believed, was brought about not only by the plan he was accused of (still in its early stages) to seize the Eastern Empire, but also by the close collaboration he had with Alaric, king of the Goths. Against the will of the entire council, he'd made a shameful treaty with Alaric that Lepidus (who was particularly opposed to it) characterized as not so much a peace agreement as a pact of servitude that obliged the emperor to pay tribute to the Goths in the guise of a pension.

DANGEROUS ADVICE

A courtier must be careful to avoid giving counsel the outcome
of which may be doubtful or dangerous. If the project is a success the prince will take the credit, but if it is not, the advisor
will take the blame. The common man judges the value of any
recommendation by its outcome; princes do the same and are
quick to unload the bad taste of bad advice onto the one who
gave it.

> Both before and after Stilicho's death, the peace treaty he had negoti-
> ated with Alaric was blamed on his poor advice. This is why Olympius
> (who Honorius used to overthrow Stilicho) decided to oppose it and,
> having complete authority at the time over the affairs of state, caused
> the treaty to be broken despite several reasonable compromises pro-
> posed by Alaric. His actions led his master to war, but when that
> conflict didn't turn out as he'd promised, it was easy for the eunuchs
> around the emperor to accuse him of being the author of every prob-
> lem then afflicting the state. Olympius was forced to leave court and
> flee to Dalmatia.

It is the job of a prince to make peace or declare war. If
you're a wise minister, you'll present the pros and cons of the
issue without recommending either. If you're obliged to express
a personal opinion, it's safer to recommend peace: this is generally the less dangerous and troublesome course, unless there's
some overwhelming need or some obvious advantage to going
to war.

> Jovius, who succeeded Olympius both in power and favour at the
> court of Emperor Honorius, used a typical ruse of professional advi-
> sors: feigning a desire for peace though he actually wanted the war to
> continue so he'd become even more indispensable to his leader. After
> a meeting with Alaric at Ariminum, Jovius sent Honorius the list of
> conditions that had been proposed by each of the parties, encourag-
> ing Honorius in a side letter to appoint Alaric general over his

armies so he'd be more willing to compromise on other matters. The emperor replied that he couldn't approve of giving this military command to Alaric or to any of his followers, leaving Jovius to accede only to Alaric's demand for pensions and food for the Goths. Jovius read this letter to Alaric, who was so furious that the emperor thought so little of him and his nation that he broke the treaty, leaving Jovius to return empty-handed to the emperor. Honorius, also incensed, swore never to make peace with Alaric and required his followers (including Jovius, the most willing of all) to swear the same. By this means, Jovius successfully

- offloaded blame for the lack of agreement onto his prince and Alaric,
- got into Alaric's good graces by recommending that he be made general of the imperial army, and
- obliged his emperor to continue the war, thereby making himself that much more necessary, consolidating his authority and reinforcing Honorius' favour towards him.

OTHER FAILINGS

I'd go on for too long if I tried to list everyone whose personal failings precipitated his fall from grace with his prince. Were I to do so, though, you'd notice several other failings that can have the same effects as those I've mentioned above. Since these failings are infinite in variety, I leave it to your good judgment and discretion to call them to mind and govern yourself accordingly.

THROUGH THE TRICKS OF YOUR ENEMIES

Let's look now at how you can come to lose favour or reputation through the machinations of others.

Your enemies, those who resent you and your competitors will usually use one of the three following means to put you down:

- removing you from court on the pretext of employing you elsewhere,
- casting suspicion on you or otherwise causing the prince to dislike you, or
- using naked force to make the prince exile or get rid of you.

ALTERNATIVE EMPLOYMENT

You can be sent away from court by many means and to suit many ends.

Going Willingly

Some people can be persuaded to leave willingly for an important position in some faraway place or because the appointment would enable them to help friends or family.

> During the reign of Emperor Manuel Comnenus, Styppiota used this technique to send away John Hagiotheodorita, a fellow executive whose reputation was greater than his own. Michael Paedagogus and Joseph Balsamon got involved in a disagreement, and Styppiota persuaded the emperor that he could end the quarrel by appointing Hagiotheodorita, Balsamon's brother-in-law, governor of the Peloponnese. To help his brother-in-law, Hagiotheodorita willingly accepted the position, not realizing that during his absence the emperor would become used to working without him, letting Styppiota take control of the business of the empire.

Others, finding themselves sucked into major disputes at court, will create their own plausible excuses to leave.

> Augustus' son-in-law Agrippa left and took refuge in Asia, ostensibly to settle some business for the emperor, but in fact to conceal the difference of opinion he had with Marcellus.

While Caius Caesar was alive, Tiberius, whom Caius hated, retired to Rhodes claiming he wanted to pursue his studies. To save face, he used his mother's influence to be named the emperor's lieutenant.

Being Sent Away

If you can't convince the person you want sent away to find his own reasons for leaving, you'll need to persuade the prince to give him an assignment, assuring him that nobody else would be as worthy or as capable. You can use a similar technique to induce your prince to recall someone to court from a position in some far-off place on the grounds that he's needed at his prince's side: this will lead to his being lost in the throng at court.

> A certain Apelles used this tactic to wrest the government of the Peloponnese from Taurion, pretending that the king needed him at his side while he was campaigning.

> Darius, on the same pretext and on Megabyzus' advice, recalled Hyesteus not to make use of him but to separate him from the Ionians, who held him in high regard.

If people used these tricks only to clear a career for themselves, then this approach, less damaging than many, might be tolerable. Unfortunately, though, many have gone far beyond this.

> During the reign of Emperor Constantius, Arbetio wanted to damage the reputation of Silvanus, a general of the infantry who was in great favour with the emperor. To this end, he had Silvanus given responsibility for leading the Gauls against the barbarians who were pillaging and ravaging that region. The reputation and authority that Silvanus gained on this campaign threw the emperor into a fit of jealousy and made him determined to ruin the general.

> Ursicinus, general of the cavalry under the same emperor, was sent to the Persian frontier to get him away from court. After he'd served there for ten years, he was sent Sabinianus, a worthless man with less

experience, to be his successor. When news reached Constantinople that the Persians were preparing for war, Constantinius' chamberlain, the eunuch Eusebius, had Ursicinus ordered to remain, though he was given no power to command. Eusebius' plan and that of the other courtiers who had sworn to ruin Ursicinus was to give the credit to Sabinianus should the Persians withdraw and to blame Ursicinus should they succeed in advancing. As it happened, the Persians were successful, and at the urging of the eunuchs, Ursicinus was discharged from the army and sent home.

Earlier during the reign of the same Constantinius, Ruffinus, uncle of Gallus and general of the Praetorian Guard, was sent to quell a mutiny in the hopes that he would be killed there and would never return.

Clytus complained that this same reasoning was what motivated Alexander to send him to the province of Sogdiana.

The Casting of Suspicion

The second method your enemies can use to provoke your fall from favour is to have your prince come to dislike or mistrust you. There are two approaches they can use to do this, and although they may appear contradictory, they in fact achieve the same effect. These are:

- false accusations, and
- praise.

Where false accusations are concerned, there are two considerations:

- Are they serious enough to change your leader's opinion of you?
- Will they be believed?

Your Prince's Opinion

You must evaluate anything that could bother your prince or alter his feelings about you in light of

- his interests,
- his humour, and
- the success of his affairs.

The most effective sort of slander, which has ruined the greatest of men, is the kind that causes a prince to seriously suspect someone of plotting against his person or his realm. Your enemies may manage to get him to believe an accusation that you, someone he promoted to a prominent position of authority, are betraying him, be it through disobedience, ignoring his instructions, insolent talk or mocking behaviour.

Credibility

The indiscreet words and deeds of an accused person and his servants, friends, and family can give credence to false accusations. Such slander can also gain credibility through

- the use of forged letters,
- the credibility of the people spreading the lies, or
- any preconceived mistrust the prince may have of the accused.

You may also unwittingly, without constraint or entrapment, act or speak in a way that can be used against you. I mentioned some examples of this earlier.

Then again you can be tricked into self-incrimination by your enemies, competitors or anyone else who bears you ill will, and such people will employ as many ruses as their malice can invent and they can find opportunity to use.

Setting Someone Up

One tactic detractors like this use is to advise (or arrange for somebody else to advise) the person they want to bring down to take some particular initiative, suggesting that it would be to their advantage, but to then use this very action as evidence of that person's bad intentions towards the prince.

> There was a monk-magician named Santabarinus who was cherished by Emperor Basil of Constantinople but hated by the emperor's son Leo. Recognizing this, the monk cultivated Leo's friendship to make him believe that he loved him. He succeeded so well that he was able to persuade Leo to wear a dagger when hunting with his father to defend himself if he was attacked. When the young prince agreed to this, the monk didn't miss the opportunity to slander him to his father, saying that Leo planned to murder him and that he carried a concealed dagger for this purpose. When the dagger was found on the prince, his father had Leo cast into prison and would have had him put to death had the whole court not intervened on his behalf.

> Emperor Valentinian III greatly respected Boniface, the governor of Africa. Aetius, seeking the ruin of Boniface, denounced him to Valentinian's mother Placidia, accusing him of wanting to make himself lord of Africa and advising her to recall him to court. At the same time, feigning friendship, he warned Boniface that he'd been denounced and would be recalled to court, cautioning him to take great care that his return didn't cost him his head. His warning convinced Boniface not only to disobey the empress' order but also to resist anyone who was sent against him. To this end he called on Gontaire and Geiseric, sons of the Vandal King Gunderic who were in Spain at the time for help, which in turn allowed these two Vandals to seize Mauritania. Aetius' fraudulent game was discovered, though, and to provide further proof of his guilt, Placidia permitted a duel between Aetius and Boniface. Aetius lost and was banished from court.

Samonas enjoyed a degree of respect from Leo, son of Basil, for having exposed the plotting of another Basil, a relative of the empress Zoe. Wanting to ruin Andronicus Ducas, who was advancing against the Agarenes or Saracens with Himerius Logothete, Samonas arranged for a friend of Andronicus' to warn him that the emperor had ordered Himerius to put his eyes out (a normal tactic in those days to neutralize princes and other powerful men) and to conduct himself accordingly. Andronicus believed Samonas' lie to be true, so he left Himerius and seized a castle. At this, Samonas denounced him to the emperor and arranged for an army to be sent against him, forcing Andronicus to retreat with the Saracens, the emperor's enemies.

Arbetio had made Constantinius suspicious of Silvanus but feared that the latter would be able to clear his name if he were ordered back to Rome by the emperor. To avoid this, Arbetio gave the letters of recall to one Apodemius who, arriving in Gaul, proceeded as he had been previously ordered and, instead of giving Silvanus the letters, incited him to rebellion by describing his situation as desperate. Silvanus' ensuing rebellion served to confirm Arbetio's accusations far better than the forged letters that (Marcellinus tells us) were planted by Dynamius and his accomplices.

To ruin Agrippina, Sejanus secretly arranged for her friends to inflate her hopes, causing her to act in ways that increased Tiberius' suspicions. So that she would soar higher on the wings of her ambition, he had Domitius Afer denounce her cousin Claudia Pulchra with the aim of provoking her into complaining to Tiberius. She did this in a manner typical of her excessive haughtiness, which offended the emperor. On another occasion, Sejanus had Agrippina warned to eat nothing her father-in-law gave her because was planning to poison her. Believing this at least in part, she stopped eating anything Tiberius put in front of her, further incensing and exasperating him. Later, the same Sejanus bribed some of the soldiers assigned to guard Agrippina and her children to persuade her to flee either to the German armies that her husband Germanicus had led or to appeal to the statue of Augustus and invoke the help of the Senate and people. All this to hasten the ruin of this princess.

In an earlier attempt to whet Tiberius' suspicions that Agrippina was plotting against his person and kingdom, Sejanus orchestrated a similar gambit involving the Roman knight Titius Sabinus. The affair was undertaken by four former praetors who aspired to be appointed consul by Sejanus, aware that his favour could only be gained through some evil act. The four agreed that Latiaris, who was closest to Sabinus, would lead and that the other three would act as witnesses. So Latiaris, on meeting Sabinus, made a few opening remarks and then praised Agrippina's loyalty to the house of Germanicus, pointing out how she had stuck by Germanicus during his difficulties as few others had done. Latiaris also said many good things about Germanicus and pretended great sympathy for Agrippina. Once Sabinus had shed a few tears over this, Latiaris criticized the cruelty, pride and scheming of Sejanus, including even Tiberius in his attack. This conversation being on a forbidden and treasonable topic, it immediately began to draw the two together. Thereafter, Sabinus met willingly with Latiaris, visiting him at home and freely sharing what was on his mind. This habit established, the four conspirators discussed how they could eavesdrop on these dialogues to shape an accusation. To listen behind a door, they feared, would lead either to their being seen or to their being discovered should they make some careless noise. Besides, Sabinus might suspect something if he was led close to a door as he spoke. Eventually, they decided to install themselves in the room above and strain to hear what was said through the cracks in the floorboards. This agreed, Latiaris met up with Sabinus and, pretending he'd just discovered something he had to tell him, led Sabinus back to his house. In the room picked for this purpose, he had him repeat everything they had previously talked about, and this was duly overheard by the conspirators listening above. With the listeners as witnesses and Latiaris as the accuser, Sabinus was condemned, and Agrippina and her children were placed in the custody of the imperial guard.

Senator Firmius Cato hoped to advance in the good graces of Tiberius by ruining Lybon, an ally of the house of Caesar. He persuaded this young man, who was more vain than wise, to consult seers and magicians to see if he was destined one day to become emperor. Having filled him with such hopes, Cato then advised Lybon to borrow and spend heavily, participated in all his pleasures and diversions and saw to it that he did all these things very publicly, giving Cato the evidence he needed to back the accusations he intended to make. Once he had enough witnesses, using the knight Flaccus as an intermediary, he denounced Lybon to Tiberius.

Even Styppiota, who so skilfully had his friend John Hagiotheodorita sent away to make himself sole manager of the realm under Manuel Comnenus, couldn't avoid being outwitted just as Sabinus had been. Camaterus Logotheta told the emperor that Styppiota was a lying charlatan who planned to betray Sicily. To lend a semblance of truth to this claim, he had the emperor hide in a special place in his house from which everything that was said in a particular room could be heard. Camaterus, bringing Styppiota to this room, steered the conversation to the topic of Sicily. Styppiota spoke carelessly, and the emperor overhead many things that made him suspect Styppiota. Camaterus was still not satisfied, so, adding ruse upon ruse, he had several forged letters interspersed into Styppiota's ledgers and papers. When these were shaken in the presence of the emperor, the letters fell out, and all this led to Styppiota's being sentenced to have his eyes put out.

Forged Letters

This example leads me to the topic of counterfeit letters, another means that many have used to add credibility to a slander. Although such forgeries are usually brought to light in the end, they can still be very effective. The suspicion they can generate in the mind of a prince will often be enough to alienate him from the accused, who is then forced either to

- withdraw quietly from court business for fear that worse might follow, or
- resort to extreme measures to protect himself, which will appear to confirm his guilt and will ultimately end his relationship with his prince: this is what happened in the example of Sylvanus mentioned above.

False Witnesses

Perjury by false witnesses can also make an allegation seem believable, even in the case of crimes such as lese-majeste and treason where additional evidence is necessary. Domestic servants serve this purpose more convincingly than any others.

> Eutropius wanted to ruin Emperor Arcadius' old captain Timasius, a man who'd built great authority and reputation. To this end he bribed Timasius' friend and close companion Bargus to accuse him of plotting against the state. The friendship between Bargus and Timasius made the accusation more credible, because nobody believed that Bargus would denounce a friend he'd so loved and aided unless he was really guilty. Eutropius went on to bolster the accusation with a number of counterfeit memoranda, with the result that this fine man and his son were exiled to the Isle of Oasis, never to return.

> Tigellinus wanted to displace C. Petronius, who was better suited than he to support Nero in his caprices. He bribed one of Petronius' servants to accuse his master of conspiring with Scevin (who had previously participated in a plot against the emperor) and thus engineered his downfall.

Credible Slanderers

The more credibility an accuser has in the mind of a prince, the more readily his accusation will be believed.

> This is why Sejanus, wanting to convince Tiberius' mother Livia of the ill will of Germanicus' widow Agrippina, bribed Livia's confidant Julius Posthumus to help him. This man was sleeping with the powerful Mutilia Prisca, his mistress, and could persuade her to manipulate Livia's thinking.

Slander is never more easily believed, though, than when it's used against someone a prince already mistrusts. Many have exploited this fact, not only to drag down someone they've accused but also to insinuate themselves into the good graces of a prince.

> Vitellius' courtiers didn't begin to defame Blaesus until his influence declined and the emperor seemed to become suspicious of him. They then lent credence to their accusations by having them delivered by Vitellius' brother.

135

Caesar's freedman Grapius, described by Tacitus as an old and refined courtier, denounced Cornelius Sylda, who Nero mistrusted, to maintain his own favour with the emperor.

Tigellinus used a similar tactic against Plautus and Sylla.

Arbetio used the same trick when he spoke poorly of Ursicinus, general of the cavalry, who Emperor Constantine mistrusted because he was related to Gallus. But since he could not prove his accusations, Arbetio chose to act as if he wanted to rescue Ursicinus, postponing his sentencing, thus leaving things up in the air. In this way, he scored three points in his favour:

- His feigned kindness placed Ursicinus, who would have feared a sentence as excessive and corrupt as were many at that time, in his debt.
- He achieved his principal objective of driving a man more honest and capable than himself out of public business and away from court.
- He reinforced the prince's suspicions of Ursicinus, while appearing to the latter as though he was working to protect him.

Factual Slanders

Reports that someone spoke ill of a prince are more believable when the actions criticized are known to have taken place.

When Cepio Crispinus wanted to accuse Geranius Marcellus of attacking the behaviour of Tiberius, he accused him of having denounced Tiberius' most disgusting and most reprehensible vices. This was believed more readily because everyone knew that all these foul habits were real.

This technique was popular with Crispinus' contemporaries, who realized that by putting words into the mouths of others, they could reproach their emperor to his face, which he would never otherwise have had to listen to.

Tiberius hated being criticized but loved to denounce others: to avoid having to listen to criticism in the Senate and to satisfy his cruelty by denouncing others, he finally decided to leave Rome and operate from Capri.

The only safe way to reproach a tyrant for his wrongdoing is to accuse someone else of having reproached him for it. It was for this reason that those who wanted to condemn Nero for murdering his mother accused a third party of having put this about; the accusation was not so much to engineer that person's death, but as a way of criticizing the tyrant.

These are the most common ways to use slander, but you must also keep a vigilant watch for any other tricks that ill will may invent, depending on the prevailing circumstances and the inclinations of your prince.

False Praises

Let us next consider the use of praises, which your enemies can use to do you no less harm than slander. Many have used compliments to disguise their hatred, envy or jealousy of another, allowing them to more easily trick the one they seek to betray.

> Fabius publicly praised Martius Valeus, the better to disguise how he was secretly criticizing him to Vitellius.

> According to Marcellinus, Arbetio saluted Visicinus as a valiant man while at the same time blackening his name to the emperor.

> Alfonso, the king of Aragon, observing one of his men lauding a companion more than was customary, remarked to one of his favourites that all that praise would likely ruin the recipient. And he was right: six months later, the same person denounced the man of whom he had formerly spoken so highly and would have succeeded in destroying him had the king not dismissed the accusation.

> Mucianus did the same to ruin Antonius Primus, praising him in the Senate shortly before disarming him.

Be warned that not only courtiers but sometimes even princes use such dissimulation when they want to destroy someone.

When Tiberius decided he wanted to engineer Libon's death, he made him praetor and graced him with extraordinary consideration, inviting him to his table and never betraying by word or deed his dissatisfaction with him.

Domitian was never more to be feared than when he was smiling.

Nicetas observed that the praises of Andronicus were the forerunners of accusations, his generosity a sign of impending confiscation, and his gentleness a harbinger of death.

Others have used praises to incite their princes' jealousy of those they praise.

Those who praised Julius Agricola to Domitian were using this strategy, to which Tacitus partially attributes the disgrace of his father-in-law.

The emperor Julian wrote to Basil that there are no greater enemies than those who use such flattery at court and that he had experience of what Mamertin said in his *Panegyric*.

Polybe wrote that in his day this was a new trick at princely courts. Envy played its games in secret and flattery in the open.

There is another way to use praises to damage someone: by praising one person to blame and blacken the name of another.

Plutarch accuses Herodotus of using this malicious technique when he congratulated the Athenians for standing up to the Persians, saying that he intended thereby to blame the other Greeks for not having done so rather than to honour the Athenians.

Seneca says that kings regularly praise the services of the dead to embarrass the living.

When the vices of his daughters were discovered, Augustus glorified the faithful service of Maecenas and Agrippa, insinuating that those close to him had lacked concern for him and his reputation.

This same Augustus used both excuses and praises to suggest what he felt was amiss. When he gave Tiberius the powers of tribune, he wrote to the Senate recommending him in fairly honourable terms, but adding several things he felt to be unacceptable and, by making excuses for Tiberius' faults, actually appeared to be criticizing him.

All of which shows that you must try as hard to understand the real intentions of anyone who praises you or seems to excuse your failings as you would those of anyone who talks ill of you.

REMOVAL BY FORCE

The final means your adversaries may use to put you down is force, which can only be used when public discontent with your advancement or behaviour is great enough to trigger either

- a groundswell of popular feeling, or
- sedition or revolt by the armed forces.

> The popular emotions that ran riot in Paris during the imprisonment of John are well known to all, as is the ill fortune of anyone who held an important office during the regency of his son.
>
> Not long ago, the scheming of the Janissaries denied the Turkish emperors their most trusted favourites.
>
> Stilicho wanted to eliminate Ruffinus, who managed all of Arcadius' affairs, so he sent Gainas to him with a few troops on the pretext of reinforcing Arcadius' army. He gave the soldiers secret orders that when Rufinus appeared before them with Arcadius, they were to wait for a signal and then fall on him and cut him to pieces, which they did.
>
> Shortly thereafter, Ruffinus' successor Eutropius upset a number of important people. Gainas contrived for Tribigild to raise a rebellion, pillaging and sacking Asia with his troops until, at the price of Eutropius' head, an agreement was reached with the emperor. Gainas was the mediator in this matter, having stayed at court so that he would be better placed to play this game. Later, this same Gainas openly revolted and joined Tribigild, and, having an agreement with Arcadius, demanded that Aurelius Saturnius and John Chrysostom

(then the emperor's chief executive) be handed over to him to do with as he pleased. When this was done, he contented himself with banishing them, but not before he had made them feel the point of his sword.

THROUGH THE ILL WILL OF YOUR PRINCE

The bad character of a prince will sometimes cut short the good fortune of those who serve him, particularly if he is

- flighty and inconstant,
- covetous,
- vain,
- cruel, or
- suspicious,
- timid.
- prone to envy,

Such flaws will generally overwhelm all the prudence a man can bring to bear to maintain his position.

> Seneca was reputed to be a wise and judicious courtier, but his student Nero's bad character defied all his courtly skills, and he couldn't prevent Nero from being jealous of his eloquence and riches. This jealousy, magnified by the pernicious comments of his enemies, cost Seneca first his power and in the end his life.

DISTRUST AND ENVY

Many have so feared being the target of their prince's suspicion and envy that they've preferred to reduce their personal profile at the expense of their leader's best interests. They've opted for this rather than risking personal ruin through raising their profile by doing the right thing.

> Ventidius, fearing the envy of Antony, under whose authority he was waging war, stopped at three victories, pushing the Parthians back to Medea and Mesopotamia without pursuing them further, even though he could have done so.
>
> Agathias tells us that Belisarius did the same thing during the reign of Justinian—driving out his enemies without pursuing them for fear that, were the reputation of his exploits to grow, the envy of the most powerful players at court would awaken that of the prince and that this envy would be compounded by the applause and rejoicing of the common people.

In truth, such behaviour betrays both your honour and your prince, but the fault must be imputed more to the master than to the minister.

It was for this reason that Maecenas counselled Augustus neither to blame his ministers when things went badly nor to envy them when things went well, so that they might focus all their energies without fear on protecting his interests. Many people in positions of responsibility, he continued, afraid of provoking the jealousy of their leaders, had preferred to do the wrong thing rather than the right, favouring the security of the former over the potential glory of the latter.

Honour to Your Leader

Personally, I applaud more the approach of those who, to avoid the burden of jealousy that comes with achieving great things, have conferred all their honours on their leader, whether he was present or not.

> Agrippa, Augustus' son-in-law, would undertake risky ventures while leaving the crowning glory to his prince, and advised others to do the same.
>
> Josephus says that Joab did this when he had Rabatham under siege, and he waited to take the city until the king himself arrived.

Craterus did likewise for his leader Alexander, waiting for him to arrive to accept the surrender of Artacena.

Agricola attributed all the glory for his own exploits to his captain.

An Affliction of Leaders

This envy or jealousy (for in this case, both produce the same effect) is a sickness common to all princes, and even the most courageous, like Philip and his son Alexander, have fallen prey to it. But there are some who succumb more readily than others.

> Emperor Theodosius II named Cyrus as his superintendent to build a wall around Constantinople that would stretch from one sea to the other. Cyrus completed the work in sixty days, and the beauty of this wall combined with the speed with which he'd met the people's need so overjoyed the populace that the word in the streets was that Constantine had built the city and Cyrus had renewed it. When this reached the emperor's ears, he summarily dismissed Cyrus and forced him to become a monk; a fine reward for having followed his leader's orders so promptly.

It's far harder to deal with people like this than it would be if they didn't allow themselves to be so easily carried away by their imagination and fears. You must try particularly hard to recognize and penetrate these tendencies in your leader so you can defend yourself against them. Even if this proves impossible, at least you'll have the consolation of knowing that you neglected nothing that your skill and dexterity could have countered.

THROUGH YOUR PRINCE'S DEATH

You'll be considered very fortunate if you're able to transfer your favour from the prince who promoted you to his successor. This happens only rarely, since those who are elevated to this degree are usually obliged in the normal course of business to oppose the presumed successor and clash with him on many issues. He who reigns usually mistrusts the person likely to succeed him so much that, far from loving him, he most often regards him with deadly hatred.

Even when this is not the case, someone who takes over a state will have his own followers, whose loyalty is better known to him than that of others. As a general rule, he will decide to promote these subordinates rather than retain the ones his predecessor favoured. Even if he doesn't, his followers will try to take the old guard's place and push them out.

THE SUCCESSFUL FEW

The few who have managed to retain their positions with a new leader have done so either

- because circumstances at the time made their particular services useful, or
- because they got into the good graces of the successor by performing some welcome service and (as the saying goes) "admiring the rising sun."

> Macro even offered the sexual services of his own wife in his attempts to get into Caligula's good graces, for whom he also, it is said, performed the service of hastening the death of Tiberius.

> Arbetio made himself so indispensable that Emperor Julian retained him in his position of power and authority, even though he in fact disliked Arbetio and knew him to be both aggressive and quarrelsome. Arbetio was subsequently called on by Valentinian to oppose Procopius.

FOR OTHER REASONS

If you reflect on all these examples, you can easily identify several things to avoid if you're to keep from falling from your leader's favour. But the most useful advice I can give to someone well placed is to appear as insecure and humble as possible towards his prince.

In deciding how to act, give more weight to how things are going for your prince than to the state of your own fortune. Do nothing to show off, do everything out of obedience and do things in a simple way to avoid kindling his envy. It is for this reason that many of the great men of history have pretended to be absorbed by debauchery or study, to show how far they were from any thought about state business.

> Domitian and Galba did this for a while during the time of Nero, affecting idleness and giving all the glory to their leader if either of them did anything of note.

Be Alert

Above all, don't allow yourself to be lulled to sleep by false praises and outward appearances. You have to stay alert to divert the calumnies and tricks that your opponents may aim at your prince or others who may rely on you.

Your Failings

Slanders based on your failings normally make much of

- some character defect people associate with you,

- something you've said to offend someone that others consider inappropriate, or
- some wrong you've done to another.

The character defect that others see in you must be

- corrected,
- apologized for personally or through your friends, or
- offset by some other attribute.

You must be sufficiently discreet that nothing you say or do can be misinterpreted by those around you. Before opening up to anyone, be sure you understand their motivations. If you carelessly let something slip, try to support the person you may have offended and convey through some service, or by expressing the opposite opinion at the right moment, that your intentions were good.

STAY CLOSE

If you discover that someone's been putting you down, you must stay close to the center of power.

If you don't, over time your absence will reduce the strength of affection in which you're held, and others will have time to print a stamp of truth on the lie; the truth cannot then be brought to light as quickly as it could have been earlier.

If an accusation goes unchallenged, a person more or less has to believe it, and even if he doesn't, his mind will remain divided and in doubt. Even if his instincts tell him otherwise, he'll still have doubts once your accuser has sworn and guaranteed that what he says is true.

If the idea is allowed to mature in the heart of a prince to whom the tale is told, his mistrust will grow, and this will prevent him from seeking out the truth as soon as he might have otherwise. His relationship with the accused will then degenerate to estrangement, and from there to dislike.

HAVE FRIENDS

If you're going to be away from court, you must of necessity find one (or preferably several) friends to defend you against any false accusations during your absence.

The friends you choose must have both access and influence and must be prepared to help you in this way. I admit that such friends are rare at court and difficult to find, everyone being quick to criticize a colleague or claim to have heard him criticized. Nevertheless, you can sometimes find someone willing to do this for you, either

- because he's in your debt,
- because he wants to oblige you, or
- because of the envy or malice he may bear towards the person putting you down.

DON'T BOAST

I've already said you should never act ostentatiously, and I repeat this to help you avoid the envy of your colleagues as well as that of your prince.

> It is written that in Spain, one of the methods the courtiers of King Philip II used to get rid of Cardinal Spinoza was for all of them to follow him about attentively and show themselves to be dependent

on him to the point that even the prince's domestic servants followed only Spinoza's orders. When the king realized this, he exiled Spinoza from court and within two years, thanks to this manoeuvre, the cardinal's fortune was destroyed.

From this you should learn to be content with as modest a train of attendants as your prince finds suitable given your status, or fewer still. Don't wait for an ebb in your fortunes to cut back on your entourage.

> It did Seneca no good at all once he'd lost Nero's favour to retire home and pretend to dedicate himself to his studies or to say that he was ill or to keep regular visitors away.
>
> Nor did it help Agricola under Emperor Domitian to go out only at night with a small company of followers.

Come to terms with modesty early in life.

CREATE OBLIGATIONS

On the other hand, it's important to use your time in favour to make as many people indebted to you as possible; not for the hollow pleasure of creating followers, but so that your fall from grace may be softened by others willing to help you back onto your feet.

It's generally considered very difficult to make friends at court who'll help you when you run into trouble. Nevertheless, out of so many people it's often possible to find at least one who'll pity your predicament and help you, if not out of friendship, then because he hopes to gain in the future from the access he establishes to you today.

DISPENSE FAVOUR WISELY

Though it will be of great advantage to you in the future (and a way to soften your fall in times of misfortune) to have used your favour with the prince while you had it to intercede for your friends, you must proceed with caution.

A Favour to You

If your prince performs a favour for someone at your request, he'll consider it to be a favour done for you. Unless your prince's attachment to you is very great, your first concern should be to keep whatever credit you have for yourself. Petition him on behalf of others only rarely, and then only on matters with which he is at least somewhat familiar, for he may hold you personally responsible for the errors of others.

Be Reasonable

You must also ensure that any favours you ask of your prince are
- fair,
- fitting given the prevailing circumstances, and
- normal for him to grant given his honour, benefit or pleasure.

Appreciation and Discretion

If your prince grants you a favour, you must show him you appreciate it greatly, and if he refuses, you must show him in any way you can that you're not dissatisfied.

Nor must you make a loud show of a prince's favour towards you, much less boast, as some have done, that your leader is managed by you. Princes want to be seen as doing things them-selves without help or direction, and certainly not through the intervention of another, least of all a subject.

Anyhow, most of such braggarts are only selling smoke.

CONFIRM INSTRUCTIONS

If a prince orders you to do something or entrusts you with some commission, try to get this confirmed in writing: include all the things you think are likely to happen and all the operational dif-ficulties you anticipate.

If the task is given to you in secret and can't be put in writ-ing, you should go over your instructions frequently with the prince. This will help you understand his objectives, and the rep-etition will make it more likely in the future that he'll remember the orders he gave you.

ACCEPT ANY TASK

You must refuse no task nor any commission from your prince, however small: minor matters have often opened the door to great fortune. Princes judge the importance of their instructions not by the intrinsic significance of the task but by their own grandeur: they are no less incensed by a refusal to take on some-thing trivial than they are by a refusal to do something of great significance.

BE PREPARED

Always be on your guard around a prince to avoid being sur-prised. To ensure you're prepared

- anticipate as best you can what he may want to talk to you about,
- prepare for everything already underway,
- speak little and only on topics you know well,
- listen when the prince speaks, and show him that your mind is not elsewhere, and
- appear neither sad nor pensive because these could be misinterpreted as criticism or dissatisfaction.

HANDLE COMPLAINTS CAREFULLY

If a malcontent comes to you to get things off his chest, hear him out once and sympathize with his misfortune.

- Encourage him and give him hope for better days.
- Deemphasize the seriousness of the wrong he thinks was done to him.
- Make excuses for the prince.
- Exhort the malcontent to keep quiet and be patient.

Proceed With Caution

Above all, be careful about what help you offer people like this. Most of them purposely invent wrongs and grievances to see if they can draw any evidence of ill-will towards the prince out of you, hoping to use your words to ruin you. Even if they're genuinely upset, they'll usually be carried away by emotion and unable to keep anything you say to them secret.

Behaviour of Servants

Great men must instruct their servants to speak modestly and soberly of both the prince and those close to him; the master is often blamed for the loose words of the servant.

SIGNS OF DECLINING FAVOUR

The greatest wisdom lies in anticipating a fall from grace or a cooling of a prince's affection. This will allow you to disengage very gently without creating a rift so that if your prince changes his mind, a door will remain open for your return. Show no sign of having taken offence or even that you've noticed that his affection for you has cooled.

The Reasons for Favour

To judge how long you may expect to enjoy the favour of your prince, beyond what you may guess by observing his humour and the changing fortunes of your friends and enemies at court, you should consider why your leader loves you. Should the original cause of this attachment disappear or should your leader find someone else he feels to be equally or better endowed with the qualities he values in you, his affection for you will certainly diminish if not cease altogether.

Often, however, you may be hard-pressed to divine the reason for your favour, and many have found themselves unable to account for their good fortune. Usually, though, a prince will favour you because

- you share the same temperament and your grace or manner pleases him,
- he feels indebted to you for services rendered,
- he sees you as a suitable personal instrument to carry out his wishes, or
- he recognizes in you some unusual qualities or abilities.

Kindred Spirits

Favour that your personal grace or manner attract, although it may appear to be completely secure, is in fact the quickest to fade. Nothing is more fickle than the humours of men, which as I have said, change not only with age, but with any small accident of business. No two people are so alike in temperament that there is nothing that differentiates them, and once a difference surfaces it separates them and pulls them further apart than when they met.

This said, I admit that the favour a prince feels for a kindred spirit is greater than any prompted by another cause. But he who finds himself thus blessed must manage his time well and put it to good use: as though sensing the onset of a storm, he should hurry to get his harvest into the barn before the rain comes.

Women

Such favour is even more violent than that enjoyed by other kindred spirits when directed towards women, when a prince's pleasure and the fury of his desire combine. But if the bad behaviour that is characteristic of such women doesn't split them up, then his having his fill of her or the arrival of a beauty he finds more attractive soon will.

Knowing this, a woman who wants to remain a favourite will usually try to distract her prince from consorting with anyone else and to keep him away from any woman who could diminish her appeal. Other women have played hard-to-get, while bolder ones, once they see that their prince is attached to them, have kept him under their thumbs.

Poppaea practised a professional trick of such women on Nero once
she had successfully made him fall for her. She pretended she wanted
to return to her husband Otho, saying that it was her duty as a wife
and that he deserved her more than Nero, who usually slept only
with chambermaids. When Nero put off divorcing Octavia for fear
that Agrippina might think badly of him, Poppea mocked him and
called him a schoolboy who was not only not an emperor but not
even a free man.

There are princes of this humour who are kept panting
more successfully by this sort of artifice than by easy access to
sensual pleasures and sex. Despite all this, the promiscuity of
such princes usually leads them to turn elsewhere.

PERSONAL SERVICES

You'd think that favour resulting from successful personal services would last longer than favour won in other ways, for it is
more honourable and can awaken many others to the prince's
service. On the contrary, however, there is no favour less durable, and often the greatest services—ones that can never be
repaid—will attract more disfavour than favour.

It's normal for princes to want to be free of any kind of debt.
Debts are a burden to them, but they are particularly bothered
when people might think they're indebted to a subject for some
signal and special service. They will avoid even meeting with
someone who has served them well, for fear that they might be
reproached for their inappropriate behaviour and ingratitude.

I regret to say that most often there is no one so held back
or so unfortunate as this kind of follower.

Just Reward

An honourable courtier avoids demanding a reward the moment he has completed a service for his prince for fear of appearing to have sold the service rather than to have performed it freely.

Besides, it is not a priority for most princes to reward their servants. Even those who acknowledge they have a duty to do so put it off to a later date and let the memory of the service fade in the minds of those who witnessed it, thus letting it be forgotten little by little.

This is why some people have decided, as the saying goes, to strike while the iron is hot. Anticipating that they'll inevitably be recruited for some venture and wanting to profit from it, they've obtained some compensation from the prince before the event. The hope of a service yet to be rendered is more powerful with princes than the fruits of a service already performed.

Many hold that it's better to be indebted to your leader than to have your leader indebted to you. A prince is better disposed towards those he has helped and he believes have good reason to think well of him than towards those for whom he's done little or nothing. He knows that, having deserved a reward but never having received one, such people have little reason to love him. This, Commines tells us, was the opinion of Louis XI.

A PERSONAL INSTRUMENT

The favour in which a prince holds those who support him in his passions and inclinations will usually last for as long as he remains possessed by the same passions and inclinations. But as he falls from one passion to another, his instruments and companions will change accordingly. Sometimes, remembering the responsibilities of his position, he will become disgusted with every habit that works against these obligations and will turn his back on anyone he associates with these habits. Nevertheless, since some passions are more durable than others, the favour of those who support their prince in any particular passion will last for a longer or shorter time accordingly.

I will not mention several of the pleasures by which princes normally allow themselves to be transported, as these rarely serve as a foundation on which to build great fortune. I will, however, outline the three excesses to which most princes surrender, namely

- lust,
- cruelty, and
- avarice.

Lust

As far as lust is concerned, the more it is violent, the less it is permanent. And even if this passion should endure in a prince, it will seldom be directed for long towards the same object.

Nevertheless, an infinite number of people have relied on lust as a stepping stone to fortune, some going so far as to offer the sexual services of their own wives.

> Otho prostituted his wife in an attempt to win Nero's favour, but the attempt backfired when, out of jealousy, Nero banished him.

Cruelty

Others have believed they could bind their princes to them the way Tigellinus did, by participating in, witnessing and encouraging thousands of evil and disgusting acts. Such people don't stop to think that a prince always has power enough to wash his hands of the envy and hatred that such excesses attract and that they're setting themselves up as scapegoats to be abandoned and sacrificed to public opinion.

> Caesare Borgia did this as well as anyone. He offloaded the hatred generated by the many cruelties that Remirus d'Orco had perpetrated on his behalf by putting Remirus to death and blaming everything on him.

The favour that someone can earn by becoming the executor of a prince's cruelty is short-lived and leads those in this profession to ruin. Not only is the prince a witness to the cruelty, but he comes to mistrust whoever was so quick to do his bidding.

> Even Nero, who was addicted and hardened to cruelty, never wanted to set eyes on Anicetus after this man had murdered his mother for him; Anicetus' presence alone was enough to accuse him of the matricide he'd ordered.

Avarice

Of all princely excesses, avarice lasts the longest. Neither age nor the variety of things coveted can make it change the way lust can change; on the contrary, avarice increases as the age of a prince increases.

Avarice is just as odious as cruelty to the common people, but they will endure it longer because of the excuse of public need, which is usually used to justify increased taxes and reduced public expenditures. It seems that those who support their prince's avarice remain in favour longer, provided that they

- use moderation, not acting too loftily or arrogantly (rare among such people who often add insult and injury to their responses and refusals), and

- don't become excessively rich themselves.

Arrogance

With respect to the first concern, acting arrogantly will usually generate public hatred, which can compel your prince to dismiss you—or worse—for fear that this hatred might rub off on him.

Excessive Riches

As for the second concern, excessive enrichment will generate envy, not only in the common man, but also sometimes in the prince himself. If he's really covetous, you must expect that, like Vespasian, he'll not stop when he has squeezed the last drops from the sponge but will do as peasants do with their swine: fatten them up to eat them later.

Our France has seen several men like this who, either because of their insolence or because of public envy of their too quickly accumulated wealth, fell at one blow from a great fortune to misery.

> Peter Berchius, high chamberlain and treasurer of France for King Philip the Fair, was hanged and then strangled in Paris. Under Philip's son Louis, Enguerrand de Marigny fared no better. Under Charles VII, the Sieur de Guyac (also high chamberlain) was sewn into a sack following his trial for the same crime and thrown into the river to drown. His successor Camus de Beaulieu was killed at Poitiers, and the same fate would have befallen Pierre des Essarts under Philip I had he not ransomed his life with a hundred thousand florins.

I will spare the memories of several others whose names I could add here. Suffice it to say that it's very important to avoid taking so many liberties in performing your duties that the prince's interests suffer. Avoid the outward displays of insolence that can attract its usual companion, hatred.

It is not forbidden to profit from your services (indeed, this is the most honourable way to enrich yourself), but you must avoid excess if you are to deter jealousy and maintain your position.

Unusual Qualities

When you owe your favour to some unusual aptitude or ability, you must understand whether your leader values this quality in you because

- he needs it, or
- he enjoys and shares your interest.

Necessity

There's no doubt that for as long as the princely need continues so will your favour, but this will be more out of necessity than out of friendship.

Common Interest

If your prince enjoys and is interested in whatever you're considered particularly talented at, you must accept that as soon as he feels that your skills exceed his, he'll begin to see you in a negative light. Princes are no different to other men in this respect: they don't want to look inferior to anyone who does the same thing as they do. Even less does a master want it believed that his valet knows more than he.

> When Asinius Pollio was urged to respond to certain verses Augustus had written about him, he replied that he would certainly never write

anything to provoke the jealousy of a man who held the power of life and death over him.

When Emperor Adrian and the philosopher Favorinus disagreed on the meaning of a word, the philosopher conceded the point to Adrian. He later told his friends he was not in the least ashamed to appear less learned than a man with thirty legions under his command.

This is why the sage admonishes us not to appear too wise before the king.

For this there is no remedy. You must sacrifice your own glory and transfer it to your prince if you want to be welcome at his side. Nor is it enough for you to simply concede an argument. You must demonstrate in word and deed that you're his inferior in everything and go as far as to purposely do something inappropriate (provided it won't greatly blemish your reputation) if you think this would please him.

PREPARING FOR YOUR FALL

YOUR DESCENT

All that I have explained to this point goes to show you how
fleeting any kind of advancement at court can be: the duration
of courtly power is far from guaranteed. Consequently, the principal concern of anyone who finds himself thus elevated must be
to prepare himself for his descent.

RETIRE GENTLY

It would be courageous to fight against your decline in power
as best you could, but if there's more to be lost than gained by
doing this it's prudent to plan to retire, fighting only as the Par-
thians do: to protect their rear in retreat.

Honour and Happiness

It's far more honourable to go down slowly and leave by the door
than to wait for others to throw you out of the window. There's
more shame attached to being unceremoniously chased out than
there is to leaving in your own time on some honest pretext.

To die happy is to die fortunate, and I consider happy the
courtier who is wise enough to retire while he's still doing well.

Wisdom

There are those who don't understand such matters who say that
someone who abandons his good fortune like this in the middle
of the race doesn't deserve the position he holds and is in over

his head. Let them ramble on, but remember that in all games of chance, it's better to get out while you're ahead than when you're behind. Never bet a certainty against an uncertainty.

Risk

You rise to great fortune step by step, but once you've reached the pinnacle, you'll likely find that there are no steps leading down on the other side. So beware. What usually happens to those who are raised up so high is that the least glare dazzles them, makes them lose their footing and precipitates them into the abyss.

VALEDICTION

VALEDICTION

These are the things that have seemed to me to be worth mentioning. I have gathered them here more for your benefit than for my own, finding expression of my own lesson and hopes in these verses of Seneca:[36]

> Climb at court for he that will
> Giddy favour's slippery hill;
> All I seek is to lie still.
> Settled in some secret nest,
> In calm leisure let me rest,
> And far off from public stage
> Pass away my silent age.
> Thus when without noise, unknown,
> I have lived out my span,
> I shall die, without a groan,
> An old honest countryman.
> Who exposed to others' eyes,
> Into his own heart ne'er pries,
> Death's to him a strange surprise.
>
> D. R.[37]

A DE REFUGE BIBLIOGRAPHY

De Refuge draws on a wide selection of classical historians (as well as his own historical knowledge) to reinforce and illustrate his advice. Many of these references were newly rediscovered works that had appeared in translation during the previous 150 years and represented major additions to Renaissance and early modern knowledge.

Bibliography. French edition, Cologne, 1703

- **Agathias** Scholasticus (c. A.D. 536–582/594): A Greek historian, Agathias is the main extant source of information about the reign of Justinian I.

- **Appian** (c. A.D. 95–c. 165): A Roman historian, author of *Roman History*, which traces the ancient civilizations that ultimately became part of the Roman empire.

- Cassius **Dio** (c. A.D. 165–after 229): A public servant who held a variety of posts in the Roman empire, Dio published an 80-volume Roman history covering almost a thousand years.

- **Euripides** (c. 480–406 B.C.): One of the three great Greek tragedians, known for his progressive use of intelligent women and servants and satirical portrayals of heroes and leaders.

- **Helvidius** Priscus: A first-century Roman philosopher and statesman, distinguished by his support for the Republic and giving imperial power to the Senate, which led to his banishment and eventual execution under Vespasian.

- **Herodotus** (484–c. 425 B.C.): A Greek historian, he wrote a history of the Persian empire intended to ensure the continuing glory of the period's heroes.

- Quintus Horatius Flaccus (**Horace**), (65–8 B.C.): A Roman poet during the reign of Augustus responsible for such phrases as *carpe diem* and the *golden mean*.

- **Josephus** (c. A.D. 37–c. 100): A Jewish historian and soldier who survived the Roman conquest of Galilee in 67 and became an informer and Roman citizen. His work gives important insight into contemporary Jewish culture.

- Ammianus **Marcellinus** (c. A.D. 325–after 391): Author of a Roman history that is a continuation of the works of Tacitus.

- Marcus Valerius **Martial** (c. A.D. 40–c. 103): Best known for his *Epigrams*, which depict daily life in Rome.

- Marcus Velleius **Paterculus** (c. 19 B.C.–c. A.D. 31): Author of the *Compendium of Roman History*, which begins with the siege of Troy and continues to his lifetime. His death may have been brought about by his support for his friend Sejanus.

- Mestrius **Plutarch** (c. A.D. 46–127): A Greek biographer, best known for his work *Parallel Lives*, which chronicles the lives of famous Greeks and Romans, including Alexander the Great, Julius Caesar, Brutus, and Pericles.

- Lucius Annaeus **Seneca** (ca. 4 B.C.–A.D. 65): Political advisor and dramatist, son of Seneca the Elder, a Roman statesman. Served as an able advisor to the emperor Nero until his alleged involvement in a plot against the emperor led to his forced suicide.

- Gaius **Suetonius** Tranquillus (c. A.D. 75–after 130): A Roman historian and biographer, Suetonius gained imperial favour under the emperor Trajan and was able to dedicate himself to a quiet life of scholarship. He is well known for his only surviving work, *The Twelve Caesars*, which chronicles the lives of Julius Caesar and the eleven succeeding Roman emperors.

- Publius Cornelius **Tacitus** (c. A.D. 56–c. 120): Of northern Italian descent, Tacitus is among the most important historians of the Roman nobility during the first century A.D. Only portions remain of his two most important works, the *Histories* and the *Annals*, both of which are noted for their narrative style and unique use of the Latin language. He believed that the only way for an empire to survive was for it to have a strong, realistic leader who could unify and mobilize the population.

NOTES

These notes are intended primarily for the business reader who may be interested in more information on Eustache de Refuge, the world he worked in, and links to modern management thought. Similarly, I have suggested some current management sources that may be of interest to historians. Consequently, where possible the references lean more towards the high-level and illustrative than the primary or exhaustive, and assume that the reader has little knowledge of early modern France or advanced management theory. Unless otherwise stated, English translations from the French are mine.

Notes. Italian edition, Venice, 1621

1: Eustache de Refuge. The spelling Eustache *du* Refuge is used interchangeably with Eustache *de* Refuge in the sources.

2: Early advice on management. See, for example, Claude S. George, Jr., *The History of Management Thought* (Englewood Cliffs, New Jersey: Prentice-Hall, 1968); Morgen Witzel, *Builders and Dreamers: The Making and Meaning of Management* (London: Pearson Education, 2002), and Daniel A. Wren, *The Evolution of Management Thought*, 4th edition (New York: Wiley, 1994). For an illustration of the behavioural lessons to be learned from earlier writers, see Ann Ripin and Peter Fleming, "O Fortuna! Medieval conduct texts, the collapse of Enron, and a call for a revolution in management education," in *Management and Organizational History* (Los Angeles: Sage, Vol. 2, 2007).

3: Renaissance. Peter Malkin and Charles Cox, for example, suggest that the experimental approach to behavioural psychology may date back to the "long sixteenth century" (*Changing Behaviour at Work: A Practical Guide*. London: Routledge, 2004).

4: Courtesy literature. Virgil Heltzel adopted the following working definition of "courtesy book" for cataloguing purposes: "any work . . . which sets forth for the gentleman (or gentlewoman) first, the qualities or criteria, inherent or acquired, which he must possess; second, his formation (including his various interests, exercises, recreations, and amusements) and his education; and, third, his conduct." (Virgil B. Heltzel, *A Checklist of Courtesy Books in the Newberry Library*. [Chicago, The Newberry Library, 1942]). Good overviews of the courtesy and then civility literary genres are found in Esther B. Aresty, *The Best Behavior: The Course of Good Manners* (New York: Simon and Schuster, 1970). A classic treatment appears in Maurice Magendie, *La Politesse Mondaine et les Théories de l'Honnêteté* (Geneva: Slatkine, 1993), and a discussion of the distinction between "courtesy" and "civility" in Anna Bryson, *From Courtesy to Civility: Changing Codes of Conduct in Early Modern England* (Oxford: Clarendon, 1998). The influence of this genre even made it to revolutionary America: see Richard Brookhiser (Charlottesville: University of Virginia, 2003) on George Washington's *Rules of Civility*, or more recently Henry C. Wheelwright, ed., *Rules of Civility for the 21st Century from Cub and Boy Scouts from across America* (Washington DC: Stone Wall, 2000). This is the same tradition that gives us Robert I. Sutton, PhD's *The No Asshole Rule: Building a Civilized Workplace and Surviving One that Isn't* (New York: Warner Business Books, 2007), or George W. Jarecke and Nancy K. Plant's *Seeking Civility: Common Courtesy and the Common Law* (Boston: Northeastern University, 2004).

5: Unvarnished realism. "Du Refuge did not forget to express moral scruples, but somehow he always found a way around them" (Peter Burke, *The Fortunes of the Courtier*. [University Park, PA: Pennsylvania State University, 1995: 122]). "Du Refuge . . . consistently adopted the realistic 17th century approach to getting ahead amidst fierce competition, stripping away the idealistic presence that courtesy books and chivalric writings had so long maintained" (Aresty 98). "He doesn't settle for gleaming and ephemeral visions; he wants to succeed at court; in effect a kind of treatise of applied-psychology for the beginner courtier" (Magendie 354).

6: Absolutism. "A system of government in which the power of the sovereign is without limit." (Lucien Bèly, ed. *Dictionnaire de l'Ancien Régime* [Paris: Quadrige/PUF, 1996]).

7: "non-moral." W. Lee Ustick, "The Courtier and the Bookseller: Some Vagaries of Seventeenth-Century Publishing" in *The Review of English Studies*, Vol. 5, Ed. R. B. McKerrow (London: Oxford University, 1929).

8: Early modern era. For our purposes, Europe and the Americas between the first voyage of Columbus (1492) and the French Revolution (1789). Merry E. Wiesner-Hanks includes a discussion of the definition of "early modern" in *Early Modern Europe, 1450–1789* (Cambridge: Cambridge University, 2006).

9: Royal and princely courts. Two easy-to-read overviews are A. G. Dickens, ed., *The Courts of Europe: Politics, Patronage and Royalty 1400–1800* (New York: McGraw-Hill, 1977) and John Adamson, ed., *The Princely Courts of Europe: Ritual, Politics and Culture Under the Ancien Régime, 1500–1750* (London: Weidenfeld and Nicolson, 1999). For the classic sociological approach, see Norbert Elias, *The Court Society*, translated by Edmund Jephcott (New York: Pantheon, 1983). For the French court specifically, see Jean-Francois Solnon's *La Cour de France* (Paris: Arthème Fayard, 1987).

10: Nobles of the Robe, intendant, etc. For a description of ranks and offices in early modern France, see Bèly 1996. For an English glossary, see James B. Collins, *The State in Early Modern France* (Cambridge: Cambridge University, 1995).

11: Early modern France. For a good review of context, see Volume 2 of Roland E. Mousnier, *The Institutions of France under the Absolute Monarchy 1598–1789*, translated by Arthur Goldhammer (Chicago: University of Chicago, 1984).

12: Catherine de Medici, Marie de Medici. Leonie Frieda, *Catherine de Medici : Renaissance Queen of France* (New York: Harper Perennial, 2006), Philippe Delorme, *Marie de Médicis* (Paris: Editions France Loisirs, 1998).

13: The title "prince." See, for example, when De Refuge refers to Alvarez, principal counsellor to King John of Aragon, as "this prince" (De Refuge 1618), or to Agrippina, daughter-in-law of Emperor Tiberius, as "this princess" (ibid). It is likely that De Refuge's contemporary readers would have understood that his comments throughout the book could apply to male and female "princes" alike, and that his deprecating observations about the mistresses of princes could apply equally to the lovers of princesses and homosexual partners.

14: Biography of the author. References to the life of Eustache de Refuge are widely scattered through print and manuscript sources. The brief biography I have provided here is as comprehensive as anything to be found in one place elsewhere, certainly in English. This said, perhaps the most complete alternative source can be found in three dense pages (334– 337) of Olivier Poncet's *Pomponne de Bellièvre (1529–1607): Un Homme d'état du Temps des Guerres de Religion* (Paris: Ecole des Chartes, 1998), a meticulous and exhaustive biography of De Refuge's father-in-law.

15: Eighteenth century chronicler. Pierre Bayle, *The Dictionary Historical and Critical of Mr. Peter Bayle*, Vol. 8 (London: Knapton et al, 1734– 41), though Bayle is providing his own translation of part of the "small Preface prefixed to the third edition of his Treatise of the Court. This edition was printed at Paris in 1618."

16: Venal offices and De Refuge. During Eustache de Refuge's lifetime, many offices (such as that of *conseiller* in the Parlement of Paris) were venal, in other words, they had to be purchased. The owner was required to assume the responsibilities of the office but also gained several benefits. Ownership not only gave access to the formal and customary income earned by the position but also exemption from almost all taxes and the temporary or hereditary right of being considered noble. The value of these offices reflected the perceived present value of the tangible and intangible future benefits associated with them. They could effectively be bought, sold and mortgaged like any other capital asset: structurally not unlike the market for taxi licenses today. Access to higher offices (e.g., *maître des requêtes* or ambassador) was earned more through merit than it was later in the seventeenth century, and required royal appointment. The value of offices was rising during De Refuge's lifetime, but it had not yet reached anything like the level it would in the decades after his death. A contributing factor here was a rule change, introduced about a decade before De Refuge's death, that made it possible for these offices to become hereditary upon payment to the royal treasury of an annual percentage of their value. Eustache de Refuge was among those who strongly opposed the venality of offices. "I have had time to reflect . . . and consider the miserable state of France, which will perish because . . . of the venality of everything, even the offices of the judiciary . . . It is shameful to see young men present themselves for office before they're ready but with a big purse of gold. They acquire great positions that they can't legitimately fill, and which can't properly be filled by anyone without experience and who has had neither the time nor the patience to learn the requirements of the profession, which they enter down the chimney instead of by the door." Eustache de Refuge, *Traité de la justice*, 367, in P. J. S. Dufey, *Harangues de Michel L'Hospital, Chancelier de France* (Paris: Auguste Boulland et Cie, 1825). The most comprehensive study of the venality of offices in France in De Refuge's day remains Roland Mousnier, *La Vénalité des Offices sous Henri IV et Louis XIII* (Paris: Presses Universitaires de France, 1971).

17: Universal Geography. Eustache de Refuge, *Géographie historique, universelle et particuliè re, avec un Traité de la préséance du roy du France contre celuy d'Espagne, par feu M. de Refuge* (Paris: M. Brunet, 1645).

18: Noble and learned jurisconsult. Eustache de Refuge, *A Treatise of the Court. Digested into two Bookes. Written in French by the Noble and Learned Juriconsull and Counceller of Estate, Monsieur Denis de Refuges*, translated by John Reynolds (London: William Lee, 1622). Jurisconsult: "he who makes the law and gives advice." (*Dictionnaire de l'Académie française*, 4th Ed. mémoire 1762).

19: Duc de Richelieu. See *Memoire d'Armand du Plessis de Richelieu, évéque de Luçon, écrit de sa main, l'année 1607 ou 1610 alors qu'il méditait de paraître a la Cour*, ed. Armand Baschet (Paris: Plon, 1880), although the attribution to Richelieu is now disputed.

20: Editions, translations and variations. This listing excludes consideration of works like Nicolas Faret's *Honneste-homme,* which clearly paraphrased the *Treatise on the Court*, Castiglione and others and was really a compendium that appeared 15 times between 1630 and 1681 (M. Magendie, *Nicolas Faret: L'Honnête homme ou l'art de plaire à la court.* Slatkine: Geneva, 1970). There is probably no exhaustive catalogue of all the various editions of the *Treatise on the Court*, but the *Bibliographie des Traités de Savoir-Vivre en Europe du Moyen Age a nos Jours*, Vol. I & II (Alain Montandon, ed. Clermont-Ferrand, 1995) comes closest. For a comprehensive but still incomplete list of the printings of Book Two, go to www.treatiseonthecourt.com. For a fascinating discussion of the various rip-offs (or hypertext borrowings) of De Refuge's work,

see Ustick. In the past century the *Treatise* seems to have appeared
in print only twice before this edition, once in English in a curiously
edited version of *Arcana Aulica* with an even more curious introduction
(Gordon Tullock, ed. *A Practical Guide for Ambitious Politicians,
or, Walsingham's Manual*. Columbia: University of South Carolina,
1961), and once in a currently available facsimile edition of the first
French translation of *Arcana Aulica*, which is itself the second English
translation (Eustache de Refuge, *Le secret des Cours, ou les memoires de
Walsingham, secretaire d'Etat sous la reine Elisabeth*. Adamant Media
Corporation, 2006).

21: *Arcana Aulica*. Eustache de Refuge *Arcana Aulica: or Walsingham's
Manual of Prudential Maxims for the States-Man and Courtier*, translated
by Edward Walsingham (London: Matthew Gillyflower, 1694). For a
more complete listing of English editions, including those appearing
under different titles, see www.treatiseonthecourt.com.

22: Previous century. For example, Pérouse has suggested De Refuge's debt
to the physician Juan Huarté de San Juan's 1575 work on psychology,
Examen de ingenios para las ciencias (Gabriel Pérouse, *L'examen des esprits
du docteur Juan Huarte de San Juan—Sa diffusion et son influence en
France aux XVIe et XVIIe siècles* : Paris: Les Belles Lettres, 1970), and
Toldo has done the same, with perhaps more enthusiasm than accuracy,
with respect to Baldassare Castiglione's 1528 work on courtesy, the
iconic *Il Libro del Corteggiano* (Pietro Toldo, "Le courtisan dans la
littérature française" in *Archiv für das studium der neueren Sprachen und
Litteraturen*: Brunschweig: George Westermann, 1900).

23: Studied today in management and organizational behaviour. It will take
someone wiser than I to compile a comprehensive list of modern texts
to typify the management disciplines of which Eustache de Refuge's
Treatise might be said to be a precursor or to trace the various threads
that connect current management thinking to that of the early modern
authors. This whole field of management and organizational history
appears to be in evolution (see, for example, Charles Booth and Michael
Rowlinson in their academic but comprehensive "Management and
Organizational History: Prospects" in *Management and Organizational
History* (London: Sage, 2006). My initial suggestions, though, are to
consider certain modern authors and the similarities in their thinking
to that of De Refuge. I'd include, as overviews, Wendy Bloisi, Curtis
W. Cook, and Phillip L. Hunsaker, *Management and Organisational
Behaviour*, Second European Edition (Maidenhead: McGraw-Hill

Education, 2007) and Terence Jackson, *Organizational Behaviour in International Management* (Oxford: Butterworth-Heinemann, 1993). For an exploration of power relationships and other topics, see Donald C. Pennington, *The Social Psychology of Behaviour in Small Groups* (Hove: Psychology Press, 2002). On consulting, look to Charles J. Margerison, *Managerial Consulting Skills: A Practical Guide* (Aldershot: Gower, 1988) and David A. Nadler, "Confessions of a Trusted Counselor," in *Harvard Business Review* (Boston: Harvard Business Review, September 2005). On professional management, Delbridge, R., L. Gratton and G. Johnson, *The Exceptional Manager: Making the Difference* (Oxford: Oxford University Press, 2006.), Mintzberg, *Managers not MBAs* (London: Prentice Hall, 2004), Pedler, M., J. Burgoyne and T. Boydell, *A Manager's Guide to Self-development*, 3rd edition (London: McGraw-Hill, 1994), Schön, D. *The Reflective Practitioner: How Professionals Think in Action* (Aldershot: Ashgate, [1983] 1991), Philip Augar and Joy Palmer, *The Rise of the Player Manager: How Professionals Manage while they Work* (London: Penguin Group, 2002). On ethics, Anthony Falikowski, *Moral Philosophy for Modern Life* (Scarborough: Prentice-Hall Canada, 1998). On following, Ira Chaleff, *The Courageous Follower: Standing up to and for our Leaders* (San Francisco: Berrett-Koehler, 1995), and Barbara Kellerman, "What Every Leader Needs to Know About Followers," in *Harvard Business Review* (Boston: Harvard Business Review, December 2007). On coaching, Robert Hargrove and Michel Renaud, *Your Coach (in a Book)* (San Francisco: John Wiley and Sons, 2007). On succession, Kevin P. Coyne and Edward J. Coyne, Sr., "Surviving Your New CEO," in *Harvard Business Review* (Boston: Harvard Business Review, May 2007). In each of the above and certainly in many more, it's interesting to compare Eustache de Refuge's four-centuries-old perceptions to current theory, practise and advice.

24: Personality styles: dealing with the four types of prince. The four temperaments or humours (choleric, sanguine, melancholic, phlegmatic) to which De Refuge refers had long been a fixture of the Western worldview. Originating with the school of Hippocrates (born about 460 B.C.) and greatly elaborated on (and named) by Galen in the second century A.D., the four humours were used to indicate the excess of a particular body fluid in an individual. Such an excess could, in theory, be eliminated or attenuated through diet, lifestyle or medication, and the individual thus restored to an optimum balance. This concept is well expressed by E. M. W. Tillyard in *The Elisabethan World Picture* (London: Chatto and Windus, 1943).

De Refuge's Four Temperaments

HOT

Choleric		Sanguine	
	SO		*SO*
• imperious	• be vigilant	• nice	• treat with respect
• won't tolerate disobedience	• follow orders	• pleasure, fun	• don't talk business
	• be humble	• liberal	• don't interrupt at play
• impatient	• don't take offence	• avoids business	
• makes hasty decisions	• avoid when angry	• avoids conflict	• expect he'll delegate to you
	• don't get close	• delegates	
• doesn't ask advice	• don't try to control	• forgets wrongs	• be happy, confident
• quick to offend			

DRY   WET

Melancholic		Phlegmatic	
	SO		*SO*
• cold	• be restrained	• slow	• be inventive
• slow decisions	• say little	• mistrusts himself	• solve his problems
• secretive, mistrustful	• don't offend or contradict	• hesitant	• succeed for him
• vindictive	• be cautious	• lacks insight	• keep others away
• opinionated		• unemotional	
• ingenious			
• unforgiving			

COLD

Eustache de Refuge expressed the behavioural traits associated with each temperament along with suggestions for how to behave towards a leader in each category, in a manner similar to that of many current personality tests and training programs. To a greater or lesser extent, these currently available instruments often mimic the four temperaments as outlined by De Refuge either directly or circumstantially through the writings of psychologists such as Jung or Marston. Compare, for example, the personality characteristics in

- the DISC Personal Profile's segments (Dominance, Influence, Conscientiousness, Steadiness) from www.discprofile.com.
- Kiersey's four temperaments (Idealist, Artisan, Guardian, Rational) from David Kiersey and Marilyn Bates, *Please Understand Me: Character and Temperament Types* (Del Mar: Prometheus Nemesis, 1984).
- Myers-Briggs cognitive function types (intuitive feeling [NF], sensory perception [SP], sensory judgment [SJ], intuitive thinking [NT]). Kiersey and Bates.

These parallel the characteristics Eustache de Refuge outlines for choleric, sanguine, melancholic and phlegmatic personalities in the *Treatise on the Court*.

The extent to which current personality tests measure differences in individual temperament better than the long-standing four humours approach receives interesting treatment by authors like Annie Murphy Paul in *The Cult of Personality: How Personality Tests Are Leading Us to Miseducate Our Children, Mismanage Our Companies, and Misunderstand Ourselves* (New York: Free Press, 2004) and Jerome Kagan in *Galen's Prophecy: Temperament in Human Nature* (New York: Basic Books, 1994).

Noga Arika charts the evolution of ideas on the humours in *Passions and Tempers: A History of the Humours* (New York: Harper Collins, 2007).

25: Segmentation of organizational relationships: dealing with great nobles. Here De Refuge proposes a segmentation based on executive power (position power) and power to access the leader (personal power).

He describes the role each category of noble can play in advancing a career and accordingly, how best to interact with each type.

(see below)

Close to the Leader

Close, No Authority	*Close, Great Authority*
• can facilitate access to the leader • can put in a good word for you, defend you from slander • can point you in the right direction • can cause you great harm *so* • get into their good graces, become valued by them • try to have them recommend you to fill important positions	• close to the leader and hold offices of great authority • these are the leader's favourites *so* • court them rather than their leader • support their agendas • be very patient; it may take time to get through to them, consider approaches through their family or friends • ask them only for things they can deliver
Little Executive Power	**Great Executive Power**
• can't help you get ahead • can damage your prospects through their friends and followers *so* • cultivate relationships with them, treat them with respect • be very careful if a project requires you to oppose them • don't confront them directly	• hold offices of great authority • tend to manage the affairs of lazy or dissolute leaders • can often appoint their own staffs *so* • try to influence these men rather than their leader, since they often run things • be careful if their leader is mistrustful and always checking up on them: your support of them could be misinterpreted • treat them with respect but, when possible, support them in secret
Not Close, No Authority	*Not Close, Great Authority*

Not Close to the Leader

26: An earlier translator. Louis Boulesteis de la Contie, in *Memoires et instructions pour les ambassadeurs ou letters et negociations de Walsingham, Ministre et Secretaire d'Etat, sous Elisabeth Reine d'Angleterre. Avec les Maximes Politiques de ce Ministre, et des Remarques sur la vie des principaux Ministres et Favoris de cette Princesse* (Amsterdam: George Gallet, 1700).

27: Italian edition. Eustache de Refuge, *Trattato della Corte, del signor di Refuge, tradotto di francese in questo nostro volgare da D. Girolamo Canini d'Anghiari* (Venice: Battista Ciotti, 1621).

28: Management guru. For a working definition, see Andrzej Huczynski, *Management Gurus: Revised Edition* (New York; Routledge, 2006).

29: 1618 "official" Paris edition. Eustache de Refuge, *Traicté de la Cour, ou Instruction des Courtisans. Nouvelle Edition, De beaucoup enrichie, comme il se verra au feuillet suivant. Avec Privilege du Roy.* (Paris: Abraham Saugrain, 1618).

30: Not the work of De Refuge. The Bibliotheque nationale de France catalogue, when commenting on an early (undated) edition of the *Treatise on the Court* states that it "predates the division of the text into chapters, which appears in the 1618 edition." This matches the claim of the editor of the "much enriched" 1618 edition that it is "added to, as you see, and distinguished by chapters, with summaries and sections, to make one less burden for your memory, and certainly quite differently to how it was first printed in Holland and subsequently in this city, having being generously given me to this end by the family and friends of the author after his death."

31: Not of much interest. The editor of the 1618 Paris edition, which forms the basis for this translation, took the same approach. He states that the family and friends of the deceased author "judged that it would not be appropriate at this time to burden the text with margin notes, nor the many authorities and authors with which the work was curiously enriched, more for the benefit of scholars than those who frequent the courts of princes."

32: Primero. In French, *première*; a popular early modern card game similar to poker, the exact rules of which have been lost.

33: Access and recognition. De Refuge outlines the access paradox: the harder it is to gain access to the leader, the greater the chances of long-term success.

34: Halfway home. Presumably De Refuge is referring to the twofold task of obtaining access and then recognition. Someone who has automatic access has automatically met the first requirement, and is "halfway home".

35: Envy, emulation. Eustache de Refuge draws an important motivational and behavioural distinction between envy and emulation throughout the *Treatise*, a distinction in keeping with usage in his day. Envy *(envie)* describes the greed a person has to possess something belonging to someone else: it is destructive, spiteful and vengeful in nature. Emulation *(émulation)* describes the motivation a person has to equal or surpass someone else in talent or merit: it is a generous, noble and healthy type of rivalry. When De Refuge refers to jealousy or competition, though, it's necessary to check the context to see whether he is referring to a malignant (envy) or benign (emulation) situation, or both.

36: Seneca. The *Traicté de la Cour* ends with this quote from Thyestes' words at the end of Act II of Seneca's tragedy *Thyestes* in the original (archaic) Latin, as follows: "Stet quicumque volet potens / aulae culmine lubrico: / me dulcis saturet quies. / obscuro positus loco / leni perfruar otio, / nullis nota quiritibus / aetas per tacitum fluat. / sic cum transierint mei / nullo cum strepitu dies, / plebeius moriar senex. / illi mors gravis incubat / qui, notus nimis omnibus, / ignotus moritur sibi." The English translation that appears here is that of the English metaphysical poet and Member of Parliament Andrew Marvell (1621–1678). (*Complete Poetry*, London: JM Dent and Sons, 1984).

37: D. R. These initials appear at the end of the 1618 Paris edition and in most, if not all, subsequent editions of the original French version. They are generally assumed to signify De Refuge, whose authorship was acknowledged by 1621 (Italian edition), 1622 (first English edition) and at least by 1649 in the original French.

INDEX

This index is in two parts: a listing of the historical figures named in the *Treatise*, and a general index of themes.

"Index of People Named in the *Treatise*". This references the proper names of historical figures and authors mentioned by Eustache de Refuge. Where part of the name or title does not appear in the original text it appears in parentheses in the index, thus "Constantius (II, Emperor)". References to authors listed in the Bibliography appear in italics.

Index. Latin edition, Amsterdam, 1642

"General Index". This indexes the whole work in a summary manner. This edition, like the original, provides exhaustive contents pages by career-stage (see pp. 5-6, 40, 48-49, 82-83, 110-112, 162), so the general index is limited to major topics. References to illustrations appear in italics.

183

INDEX OF PEOPLE NAMED
IN THE *TREATISE*

GENERAL INDEX